THE BEATLES IN AMERICA

THE BEATLES IN AMERICA

THE STORIES, THE SCENE, 50 YEARS ON

SPENCER LEIGH

Consultant Editor
Mike Evans

OMNIBUS PRESS

London / New York / Paris / Sydney / Copenhagen / Berlin / Madrid / Tokyo

Copyright © Elephant Book Company Limited 2013
www.elephantbookcompany.com

Published by Omnibus Press
(A Division of Music Sales Limited)

Editorial director: Will Steeds
Senior editor: Laura Ward
Project manager: Alison Candlin
Book and cover design: Louise Turpin
Picture research: Sally Claxton
Fact checking: Mark Naboshek
Copy editor: Kristi Hein
Production: Alastair Gourlay
Reproduction: Pixel Colour Imaging

ISBN: 978-1-780388-80-9
Order No: OP55154

Exclusive Distributors
Music Sales Limited, 14/15 Berners Street, London, W1T 3LJ
Macmillan Distribution Services, 56 Parkwest Drive Derrimut, Vic 3030, Australia

A catalogue record for this book is available from the British Library.

Visit Omnibus Press on the web at www.omnibuspress.com

Printed in China

Pages 2-3: The Beatles are clearly enjoying a photo shoot in the Miami sunshine on their first visit to America, in February 1964.

CONTENTS

FOREWORD

The Beatles totally transformed popular music and it is hardly surprising that we are celebrating the fiftieth anniversary of major events in their career throughout this decade. I would contend that the most important and significant of all is the fiftieth anniversary of the Beatles conquering America in 1964.

I am both happy and proud to have played an important part in all this by presenting the Beatles at Carnegie Hall in February 1964 and then at Shea Stadium in both 1965 and 1966.

I treasure their music and I treasure their friendship, and I am delighted that Spencer Leigh is telling their story in both words and pictures.

SID BERNSTEIN, APRIL 2013

INTRODUCTION

"I don't know how it was in Britain, but in America our music was getting stale. We had suffered the Kennedy assassination, and so the Beatles were a breath of fresh air. The whole world owes them a debt, as they brought happiness to all of us."

JOSÉ FELICIANO

IN 1962 THE BEATLES' MANAGER, Brian Epstein, told his friends and associates—and, indeed, anyone who would listen—that his band, the Beatles, were going to be "bigger than Elvis." Even his brother, Clive, thought he was talking nonsense. Yes, the Beatles had talent and would most likely have hit singles in the United Kingdom, but bigger than Elvis? No, no, no. How could the Beatles be bigger than Elvis when that would mean conquering America? Few British pop acts had had more than fleeting success in the States.

Brian Epstein's supreme confidence was justified, and the Beatles' conquest of America is a remarkable story, full of highs and lows. Indeed, the group's very success in the United States and across the world was also a primary cause for their breakup.

Prior to their success in the United States, the Beatles were already riding high in their native United Kingdom and elsewhere in Europe. They had developed their sound in Liverpool clubs and

Right: Ed Sullivan with the Beatles on February 9, 1964. His approval helped their success in America, and can be contrasted with Dean Martin's disdain when he introduced the Rolling Stones later in the year. Long hair wasn't for him, but, paradoxically, his displeasure helped the Stones.

dance halls and in the St. Pauli district of Hamburg. In October 1962 they released "Love Me Do," their first single for EMI's Parlophone label. Throughout 1963 they had a string of hit singles and two chart-topping albums, all produced by George Martin, and by early 1964 they were prepared for the challenge of America.

The Beatles were growing up fast, but they still had a youthful immaturity. They were in a Paris hotel when they heard that "I Want to Hold Your Hand" was top of the American charts, and their immediate reaction was to have a pillow fight.

NEXT STOP: AMERICA

In February 1964, the Beatles flew to America for the first time to make their debut appearances on *The Ed Sullivan Show*. Such exuberance and energy had not been seen on primetime TV since Sullivan introduced Elvis in 1956.

There was a tremendous demand for tickets to see the Beatles play live in Washington and New York during that first visit. Every news outlet was discussing the Beatles, the key topic being the length of their hair, which by today's standards would not seem particularly long. Everybody loved the levity of their press conferences, and parents, who had found the early Elvis unsavory, generally approved of their children liking the Beatles.

The music writer and social historian Greil Marcus has commented, "You did not have to love them all to love the group, but you could not love one without loving the group, and this was why the Beatles became bigger than Elvis."

Everything worked out superbly for the Beatles, and in April 1964, the Beatles held all of the Top Five slots on the U.S. *Billboard* singles chart.

When the Beatles landed in America on February 7, 1964, CBS anchorman Walter Cronkite observed in his news report that "The British Invasion this time goes by the code name Beatlemania." At the time, the British Invasion referred solely to the Beatles, but within a few months the trade paper *Billboard* was using it to describe other long-haired beat groups from Britain. The Beatles had opened the door for the Rolling Stones, Gerry and the Pacemakers, the Animals, the Dave Clark Five, Herman's Hermits, and many other acts, but none could match the Beatles' popularity.

A major summer tour covering both the United States and Canada was set up, and Epstein's team—a mixture of his British staff and American promoters—organized things perfectly. The concerts were a triumph, and even though the Beatles knew that no one could hear them above the screaming, they enjoyed the sheer novelty of the tour.

The demand for Beatles tickets was so great that in 1965 Brian Epstein, encouraged by the New York promoter Sid Bernstein, upped the ante by having the group play huge baseball and football stadiums. This was a new concept, and again the Beatles rose to the challenge. The sound systems, either the Beatles' own or the stadiums', were usually not up to the task, and although hundreds of thousands of fans saw the Beatles—admittedly in the distance, as there were no giant plasma screens in that era—not too many heard them. Sometimes the Beatles mouthed the words and nobody noticed. Nevertheless, this was the birth of stadium rock.

Although the Beatles' music was advancing lyrically, musically, and technically, they showed little inclination to play their new songs on tour, or at best they simply went through the motions. By their third North American trek, touring had turned into a nightmare, and the four Beatles agreed in August

1966 that Candlestick Park in San Francisco would be their final concert. In cultural terms, the Beatles had changed the world by that time—and the world changed them, too. The many factors which led to their eventual dissolution are almost all connected to America in some way. They include the boredom with touring; the growing influence of New York–based Yoko Ono on John Lennon; Paul's move to put their business affairs in the hands of his American wife's family of show business lawyers; the machinations of their avaricious new manager, Allen Klein; and the role of U.S. producer Phil Spector, who doctored the *Let It Be* tapes.

Above: The Beatles arrive in New York for the first time on 7 February, 1964 for a short visit of concerts and public appearances before their first major U.S. tour later the same year. Brian Epstein's management of the Beatles was already legendary and he could be photographed alongside them without people asking, "Who's that guy on the left?"

But let's start at the beginning. There is little need to devote much space within the pages of this book to discussing *why* the Beatles made such an impact when they hit America in 1964. The principal reason is very simple and often overlooked: the Beatles' music was far better than anything else that was around at the time.

1 JUST GIVE ME SOME OF THAT ROCK 'N' ROLL MUSIC

"The idea of having a hit record in America seemed ridiculous to me. That's what I thought, anyway."

JOHN LENNON

Left: The Hungarian-born photographer, Dezo Hoffmann, was a newsreel cameraman in the Second World War. He became a showbiz photographer after the war, but some of that grittiness remained, and his extraordinary picture of the Beatles on a bombsite became familiar worldwide as the cover image of their *Twist And Shout* EP.

THE AMERICAN REVOLUTIONARY WAR, which ended in 1783, may have separated the American colonies from Great Britain, but in place of that bond it generated a friendship between the two countries that even today is often called "the special relationship." During and after the war, some of those colonists who remained loyal to Britain moved north to Canada, a country that still accepted the British monarch as head of state.

One of the strongest links between Britain and America was wretchedly connected to the slave trade. When slavery was abolished in Britain in 1807, it was thought that the northwest port of Liverpool—where so many slave boats returned after dropping their human cargo in America— might lose its importance. Instead, it turned out to be ideally placed for the transportation of commodities between the two countries and for shipbuilding, too, and the port took on a new, but just as significant role as go-between. During the twentieth century, particularly up to the advent of affordable trans-Atlantic airline services, the ocean-going passenger line to New York was especially profitable. The so-called "Cunard Yanks" who worked on the liners often returned with American goods to delight their wide-eyed families and friends at home in Britain.

The American Dream, as propounded in many Hollywood films, made the country seem like the promised land. It was a magical place, with its skyscrapers; its music (jazz, crooners,

Below: Diners and drive-ins were unknown in 1950s Britain. With their shiny chrome, burgers and soda, and short-skirted waitresses—sometimes even on skates—they epitomized the allure of the American Dream.

Cadillac...universal symbol of achievement

and rock 'n' roll); its beautiful, enormous automobiles (open-top convertibles, Cadillacs, and Chevrolets); its fashions (nylon stockings and leather jackets); and its technology (cameras and refrigerators); not to mention its food and drink. The Brits even envied Americans their popcorn and hamburgers, as British cuisine was still very much a meat-and-two-veg affair, and chewing gum—which became ubiquitous—was originally introduced from America.

The Irish playwright and political activist George Bernard Shaw once remarked, "England and America are two countries separated by a common language." The same language was spoken, of course, but with variations in terminology, spelling, and pronunciation, and increasingly a quite different set of cultural references. Even "the Beatles" is pronounced differently in America (more like "the Beadles"). As British teens gained greater exposure to American popular culture, they wondered: just what were *homecoming queens*, and what did the Americans give thanks for at Thanksgiving? How did truck stops, fast-food restaurants, and drive-in movies work?

Top: In the 1950s and 60s, the prestige cars in America were Cadillacs, Lincolns, and Imperials. You'd expect the pop stars of the day to have 1959 Cadillacs—and they wouldn't be washing them themselves!
Above: The comfortable, bulbous shape of Britain's ubiquitous Morris Minor was a far cry from the tail fins and sharp lines of the vehicles being driven on the other side of the Atlantic. There were two models—the saloon, and a half-timbered estate, known as the Traveller: a small and homely kind of station wagon.

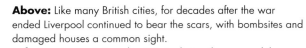

Above: Like many British cities, for decades after the war ended Liverpool continued to bear the scars, with bombsites and damaged houses a common sight.

Left: Americans stationed in Britain during the war and the following years embraced the local culture. These four servicemen enjoying a British beer outside a village pub in June 1942 were among the first U.S. troops on British soil.

The literature too, made America seem unattainable. Jack Kerouac's *On the Road* (1957) may resemble the flip side of the American Dream, but it was equally enticing to more rebellious British teenagers. In the United Kingdom, a road trip was hardly an odyssey, as you were never far from home, but in the United States there were vast areas to be covered. American comics too were vastly different from British ones—Superman and Batman had a coolness that UK characters like Desperate Dan and Lord Snooty somehow lacked.

The Americans viewed the United Kingdom with both amusement and respect, and because America was a relatively new country, Americans particularly admired the British heritage. Although their country had achieved independence from its colonizer, most Americans were fascinated by the monarchy and the antiquated peerage with their stately homes. They loved actors who spoke the "Queen's English," like David Niven, Laurence Olivier, Vivien Leigh, and Richard Burton. A thoroughly British entertainer, Noël Coward, was a huge success in Las Vegas. In the United Kingdom, traditionally everything stopped for tea, and many Brits thought of Americans as brash and uncouth. So although the United States and the United Kingdom had striking similarities and a common language, there were marked differences between them, too.

MERSEYSIDE TO STATESIDE

To most adolescents growing up in Merseyside (Liverpool and its environs) in the early 1950s, America sounded more glamorous and exciting than anything the UK could offer. Britain was in the grip of post-war austerity, and in Liverpool and other big cities there were still acres of bombsites where buildings had previously stood.

During the war and into the 1950s, American servicemen were stationed at Burtonwood, near Liverpool, and were often seen in the city, enticing local girls with perfume and nylons that were hard to come by in the UK. As elsewhere, the servicemen were jokingly criticized by the locals for being "overpaid, oversexed, and over here." Many of the servicemen would go on to become parents of children who screamed at the Beatles—and because their parents had fond memories of the United Kingdom, this worked in the Beatles' favor.

Merchant seamen—the aforementioned "Cunard Yanks"—who would travel from Liverpool to New York and return home with American products undoubtedly brought back records from the United States. However, their impact on the local beat scene has been much overstated, as the American songs which the British groups covered had nearly all been released

Above: Looks nothing special but this is a study in Anglo-American relations. It's 1955 and a Community Relations Officer for the Royal Air Force is welcoming American soldiers to the Burtonwood airbase in Lancashire, a maintenance and supply base for the U.S. Air Force in Europe. The base started to wind down in 1959 and closed in 1965.

in the United Kingdom, and were available at NEMS record stores. The manager, Brian Epstein, had a policy of retailing every record released in the UK, no matter how obscure.

In 1954 George Harrison's sister Louise married an engineering draftsman from Dundee, Gordon Caldwell, and they moved to America. They settled in the mining town of Benton, Illinois, two hundred miles from St Louis and in September 1963 George and his brother Peter visited them.

George was the first Beatle to go to America, and he was able to afford the trip because of their United Kingdom success. It enabled him to get away from the mayhem of Beatlemania: nobody knew him in Benton, Illinois, although he had sent a dozen copies of "From Me to You" to Lou, and she had had them played on radio station WFRX. On George and Peter's first day in New York they visited the Statue of Liberty. On Broadway they saw the British star Anthony Newley (who had recorded "I Saw Her Standing There" for the U.S. market) in his hit show *Stop the World—I Want to Get Off*.

In Benton, Louise introduced George to a local band, the Four Vests, and George sat in with them a couple of times, playing Hank Williams and Chuck Berry songs. George was taken with Kenny Welch's solid-body Rickenbacker guitar and bought one, as they were not available in the United Kingdom. He went camping, drove a Cadillac, saw drive-in movies, and was entranced to be served by drive-in waitresses on roller skates.

"I can't tell you how much I enjoyed America," said George when he returned home, "Their standard of living is so much higher than ours in every way—they all have central heating and air conditioning and every house has a big television . . . America has everything: why should they want us?" He had asked in record stores for the Vee-Jay and Swan releases by the Beatles, without success—and came away fearing that it was going to be hard to crack America.

continued on page 26

Opposite page right: Compared with the austerity of post-war Britain, America in the 1950s and early 60s seemed a glamorous land of plenty. "America has everything," George observed after his visit, "Why should they want us?"

Opposite left: George saw Anthony Newley's Broadway hit, *Stop the World—I Want to Get Off*; the U.S. success of British imports like this encouraged Brian Epstein to try introducing the Beatles to America.

Above: In Britain, the Beatles had moved from Cavern band to major stars, and Beatlemania was already in full swing. This image is from a Granada TV program for their native north-west, but they were household names all over the country.

Right: George Harrison took home sixteen albums from his visit to the States, including a copy of Booker T & the MGs' *Green Onions* and one by James Ray, which contained "Got My Mind Set on You," which George himself recorded in 1987.

CAPITOL ISSUES

That the Beatles triumphed in America in such spectacular fashion is testament to the band's originality and their astonishingly broad appeal, but how did it ever happen?

IN 1964 ALONE, THE BEATLES HAD NINETEEN TOP 40 HITS IN AMERICA, INCLUDING SIX NUMBER ONE HITS. This is a staggeringly impressive achievement; there has been nothing like it before or since. The reason is simple: no record company wants to promote more than four or five singles by the same act in a year. What took place was saturation marketing gone berserk, and any promoter would—ordinarily—fear that the public would be turned off by such overexposure.

The songwriter Johnny Mercer was one of the founding members of Capitol Records. Largely through his connections, they established an impressive roster, and during the 1950s had huge successes with mainstream singers including Frank Sinatra, Peggy Lee, and Dean Martin. They were less successful in the teenage market, but they did have Gene Vincent ("Be-Bop-A-Lula," 1956), the Kingston Trio ("Tom Dooley," 1958), and the Beach Boys

Left: A business party in the Savoy Ballroom, New York with (left to right) John Hammond (with cigarette)—who discovered Woody Guthrie, Bob Dylan and Bruce Springsteen—two further along from him is Earl Hines, three further along Charlie Christian, opposite him at the far end on the right is jazz and blues singer Helen Humes (wearing the head scarf), two further along is Dave Dexter (Capitol Records) with his prominent high parting, two further along again, Count Basie, and finally Benny Goodman.

Right: The Capitol Records building in Hollywood; built, according to legend, to resemble a stack of records, which the architects have since denied.

("Surfin' USA" and "Surfer Girl," both hits in 1963).

EMI relied on licensing agreements with American labels to release their products in the United Kingdom. However, the American labels, having used EMI to establish a new artist in the UK, would sometimes move elsewhere to release subsequent records under a better deal. To maintain stability, in 1955 EMI bought Capitol Records for US$8.5 million and in 1957 EMI consolidated its American operations by merging EMI (U.S.) Ltd with Capitol.

So far, so good—but some key personnel at Capitol resented their new owners and simply did not want to release British product in the United States. Capitol had a surprise U.S. number one with Laurie London's "He's Got the Whole World in His Hands" in 1958, but issued Cliff Richard's UK smash "Move It" with no promotion at all. In fact, a number of major British hits were licensed to other U.S. labels after Capitol turned them down.

In 1962 Alan Livingston became president of Capitol Records. He had

had not broken their contract. Because they had not paid EMI their royalties on "I Remember You," Capitol had the right of first refusal on the next singles from Frank Ifield and the Beatles— respectively "Confessin'" and "She Loves You"; Dave Dexter chose "Confessin'" (which became a minor U.S. success), but he decided to pass on "She Loves You."

YOU CAN HEAR IT, BUT CAN YOU GET IT?

Radio stations were playing Beatles tracks, but they weren't yet in the shops in the U.S.. Singer songwriter Rodney Crowell says, "I had heard of the Beatles about a year before Ed Sullivan. There was a radio station in Houston, Texas, that had got hold of 'Please Please Me' and I heard it every morning on the school bus. The record slayed me, but I couldn't buy it. When the Beatles released their album *Introducing the Beatles*, I saw it in the shops and I knew it was the music I had heard on the radio."

Bernie Binnick, president of Swan Records of Philadelphia, had been to the United Kingdom with the label's most successful artist, Freddy Cannon, whose "Palisades Park" was released by EMI in the United Kingdom. As a result of their friendship, Swan was given "She Loves You," which *Cashbox* (a U.S. trade weekly for the music and coin-operated machine industries) described as "a robust romantic rocker." The single was played to the voting panel on Dick Clark's *American Bandstand* (also based in Philadelphia), but it garnered only a mediocre review. Nevertheless, Swan had the option for the next single, "I Want to Hold Your Hand."

Brian Epstein was dismayed that Capitol was rejecting the Beatles' strongest single to date, "I Want to Hold Your Hand," and he telephoned Alan Livingston direct. Livingston said that he had never even heard the Beatles and relied on Dexter's recommendations. Appreciating that Epstein had EMI's support, Livingston agreed to listen to the single. Dexter dismissed them as "long-haired kids," but Livingston overruled him and persuaded Swan to drop their option for "I Want to Hold Your Hand."

Brian Epstein then made an astute move: he insisted that Capitol spend $40,000 to promote the single. Livingston agreed; perhaps he thought that if it failed to sell, that would get the English off his

many years' experience with Capitol, and had cowritten their children's hits "Sparky's Magic Piano" and "I Tawt I Taw a Puddy Tat," and engineered one of the greatest collaborations in pop music when he had teamed Frank Sinatra with Nelson Riddle.

Capitol executive Dave Dexter had the task of listening to EMI's UK releases and deciding what was suitable for America. He had been with the company since the 1940s, and he liked jazz and blues. He thought there would be little interest in British acts in America, and turned down "Love Me Do," "Please Please Me," "From Me to You," and "She Loves You."

A New York lawyer, Paul Marshall, acted for both EMI and the Chicago-based label, Vee-Jay. When Capitol rejected Frank Ifield's UK smash "I Remember You," Marshall thought they had missed a good thing and tipped off Vee-Jay—in 1962 it became a U.S. Top 10 hit for them. Marshall also placed "Please Please Me" and "From Me to You" with Vee-Jay, even though they dealt predominantly with black R&B (including Gene Chandler and John Lee Hooker) and gospel music (the Staples Singers).

Vee-Jay had the rights to the UK album, *Please Please Me*, but didn't release it at the time, and their licensing arrangement also gave them first refusal on all future Beatle releases for five years. It could have been the best deal they ever made if they

back. Capitol created a big campaign around the single, largely focused on the length of the Beatles' hair, and with some of their budget they even coaxed Hollywood stars like Janet Leigh to wear Beatle wigs. The single exploded onto the charts.

Capitol released *Meet the Beatles!* (based on the second UK album, *With the Beatles*), while Vee-Jay, taking a chance, issued *Introducing the Beatles*. They were not entitled to do this, and litigation went back and forth as the album kept selling. Vee-Jay then exploited the tracks they had for all they were worth, and further albums included *The Beatles vs. the Four Seasons* and *Jolly What! The Beatles and Frank Ifield on Stage*. There was nothing live about the latter album, and in an example of careless packaging (or was it?), the compilation was referred to in the liner notes as a "copulation."

In an eccentric court decision (made on April Fools' Day, 1964), Vee-Jay was allowed to release "Love Me Do" as a single, on its subsidiary label Tollie. By the time Vee-Jay had been ordered to stop in October 1964, they had milked two million-selling albums and five million-selling singles from just sixteen tracks. They released an album of American press interviews, *Hear the Beatles Tell All*, and they had a tribute band, the Merseyboys, record an album of Beatles songs written by the Beatles themselves.

For the week ending April 4, 1964, the top five positions on the *Billboard* chart were held by "Can't Buy Me Love" (Capitol), "Twist and Shout" (Tollie), "She Loves You" (Swan), "I Want to Hold Your Hand" (Capitol), and "Please Please Me" (Vee-Jay). Also in the charts were a couple of singles from Capitol of Canada, and even Tony Sheridan and the Beatles' "My Bonnie" had been picked up by MGM and was selling well. The Beatles accounted for 60 percent of all the singles bought that week.

Up until that point, Dave Dexter had released hardly any British product, but he didn't admit his mistake or change his views. Songs by Cilla Black and Peter and Gordon were released on Capitol, but he passed on the Hollies and Billy J. Kramer (both Imperial), the Animals and Herman's Hermits (both MGM), Gerry and the Pacemakers (Laurie), Manfred Mann (Ascot), and the Dave Clark Five (Epic).

At nearly every stage of the Beatles' career, they were supported by first-class people who were sympathetic to what they were doing. The only instance in which it went horribly wrong was with Dave Dexter, the man who turned down the British Invasion, but even then it worked to the Beatles' advantage.

Above: In an extraordinary licensing muddle, the Beatles found their records released in the U.S. by a handful of different labels, often at the same time so that they were competing for the top positions in the charts. *Introducing the Beatles* (top) was released without proper authorization by Vee-Jay, although they did own the rights for *Please, Please Me* (bottom).

AMERICAN BYSTANDERS

During 1963, several U.S. performers toured the United Kingdom. When they arrived, they had never heard of the Beatles, but they certainly had by the time they left.

"I was on tour with my producer, Snuff Garrett, when someone played me 'Love Me Do.' We loved it and thought it sounded like a Crickets record. Snuffy got very excited and wanted to buy the rights for America, but EMI wanted $25,000, which at the time was too much money. It seemed outrageous—RCA only paid $35,000 for Elvis, and this was a new group!"

BOBBY VEE

"I played in Liverpool when the Beatles had 'Please Please Me' out, and I thought it sounded great. It was clear that they sang and played their own instruments and were involved with the whole process of making the record. This contrasted with a lot of American performers who made records with session guys they didn't even know. I did an American tour with Bobby Vee in 1963, and I remember us sitting in the dressing room on the opening night singing 'Love Me Do' and 'Please Please Me' together. The others on the tour were amazed. They'd never heard the songs before, and they thought they were great."

BRIAN HYLAND

"I was gathering songs from all around the world that I might record, and I brought an English song home—[sings] 'If there's anything that you want, If there's anything I can do.' I tried my best to get Randy Wood to let me record the song, but he said, 'No, that'll never be a hit.'"

PAT BOONE

"'From Me to You' was a big hit, and I told John Lennon that I was going to do it. He said, 'That'll be all right,' but then, just as he was going on stage at the Royal Albert Hall, he turned to me and said, 'Don't do that.' Brian Epstein had told him that he didn't want any Americans covering their songs. The Beatles were going to invade America by themselves."

DEL SHANNON

Del ignored Epstein's request, and his version of "From Me to You" marked the first appearance of a Lennon-McCartney song on the U.S. Hot 100. Also, when Del was touring the United Kingdom with Johnny Tillotson in April 1963, they sang "From Me to You" together at the Liverpool Empire.

"We could tell that they were going to be popular, and I started to learn their tunes. I also wrote six or seven tunes such as 'She's Sorry' in that fashion. It was done with the kindest of intentions, a proclamation that there was this new sound in England. It never entered my mind that I was ripping them off, although it may look like that now."

BOBBY VEE

"I am very proud to be a part of the history of the Beatles, and my memories of our tour are all great. They were getting hot in England, and it was tough following them. We turned the whole thing around, and they ended up closing the show. I was so impressed that I started doing their songs and tried to get them a record deal in the States. My record company turned them down, and I think now that they should have seen them. Their records weren't too impressive in the beginning—they were doing their take on '50s music—and you really had to see the image alongside the music. Once the Beatles started getting publicity in America, it was bound to happen."

TOMMY ROE

"I was touring England with Tommy Roe and an unknown group called the Beatles. They were booked to get the show going, and they had such energy and power. They played me their album, *Please Please Me*, before it was released, and I was knocked out. I couldn't stop singing 'I Saw Her Standing There.' It was such a great song. I was top of the charts and topping the bill, but when we got to Liverpool, I said, 'This is your town, you close the show; I'm not the headliner here.' They were amazed that I should say that."

CHRIS MONTEZ

Right top: Tour photo of the Beatles with Chris Montez and Tommy Roe. Despite their hits and higher billing on the tour, they could not compete with the screams for the Beatles.

EARLY TREMORS

The songwriter P. F. Sloan, who wrote the 1965 hit (for singer Barry McGuire) "Eve of Destruction," recalls, "I was working for a publishing company in 1963 and I heard 'Love Me Do,' 'Please Please Me,' and 'From Me to You.' They were fantastic, like putting your fingers into an electric socket. I went to the head of the company and said, 'These guys are going to be bigger than Elvis,' and the record company called up Brian Epstein and said, 'There's a kid here who says this group is going to be bigger than Elvis.' Brian said, 'I've been saying the same thing myself.' Capitol worked out a deal and the Beatles came out on Vee-Jay. They bombed terribly until 'I Want to Hold Your Hand'—then suddenly they were everywhere."

The Ed Sullivan Show was the biggest TV entertainment show in America, and from time to time he featured British acts. In September 1963 he shot a sequence with Cliff Richard and the Shadows at Elstree studios near London. It was Cliff's third appearance, and Sullivan told the United Kingdom pop paper, *Disc*, "Cliff appeals very much to the younger people who watch my show. As for the older folk, they recognize him to be a real nice, gentlemanly person—the type they would invite into their homes." As a result of the appearance, Cliff's "Lucky Lips" was a minor U.S. hit.

On October 30, 1963, Ed Sullivan and his wife Sylvia happened to be at London Airport when the Beatles were returning from Sweden. He heard the fans screaming and thought he would investigate. He was soon negotiating with

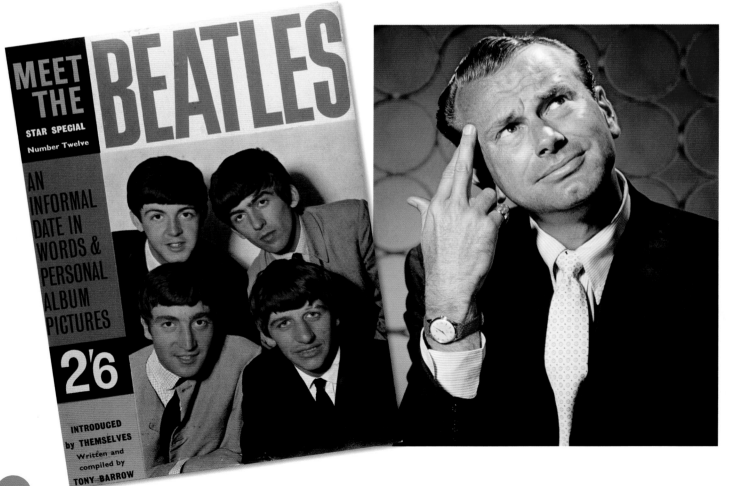

CHAPTER 1 : JUST GIVE ME SOME OF THAT ROCK 'N' ROLL MUSIC

Brian Epstein, and although he normally paid $7,500 for a major act, he signed the Beatles to perform two live shows on February 9 and 16, 1964, with a third appearance recorded for February 23, for just $10,000 overall.

The Beatles appeared in the Royal Command Performance on November 4, 1963, the famed appearance at which John Lennon told the gentry to rattle their jewelry. The NBC talk show host Jack Paar was in the audience; Paar, taking his time, broadcast a segment about the Beatles on January 3, showing them in concert in the UK, with his own supercilious commentary. "It is part of the legend that Ed Sullivan was the first who presented the Beatles in America, but this is not true," said Paar, who died in 2004. "I had them on my show

Opposite page left: There were hysterical fans wherever the Beatles played. First they took Britain by storm, then moved to Europe and America. The merchandizing reached fever pitch in America, and the British equivalent was decidedly low-key. *Meet The Beatles* was compiled by Tony Barrow, the Beatles' press officer, who coined the moniker, "The Fab Four."
Opposite page right: Posing for photographs did not come as naturally to the TV host and newsman Jack Paar as it did to the Beatles. He saw the band perform at the Royal Command Performance in November 1963, and gave them their first TV coverage in the U.S., though perhaps not quite for the right reasons . . .
Above: When Jack Paar aired a clip of the Beatles in concert on his NBC talk show, it was to ridicule their strange haircuts and the—as he saw it—bizarre overreaction of their screaming fans, not to talk about their music at all. As history proved, and Paar himself later admitted, it was a massive misjudgment. Paar just thought they were funny.

earlier, but I never knew that they would change the history of music. I just thought they were funny."

Dennis Locorriere, later lead vocalist and guitarist of Dr. Hook, remembered the Paar feature: "Before Ed Sullivan, there was a little clip on *The Jack Paar Show*, which he regarded as an oddity, you know: 'Wow, look at this freaky thing from across the ocean.' It was like he had discovered aliens. It was a pretty dark clip too. I really noticed them when I heard 'I Want to Hold Your Hand' on the radio. It jumped off the radio; the cymbals were so bright and vibrant. It made me want to play something myself—bang on a box with spoons, I suppose—but it got me going." Paar's footage of the Beatles was from their show at the Winter Gardens, Bournemouth, in November 1963.

Beatles biographer and academic Steven Stark offers this assessment: "Feminist gender bending was a feature of their music and a big part of their cultural impact. On and just before the first visit, the American press said very little about the music—it was all about their hair and how they looked like girls. Jack Paar broadcast a clip of them doing 'She Loves You,' and all the talk was about the girls screaming and their haircuts. It was a real shock, as the crew cut was the big thing in the United States, and anything longer was a big deal."

On November 5, 1963, Brian Epstein and his protégé Billy J. Kramer left a damp and dismal London and flew to New York. "It was wonderful," says Billy. "It was like the world

  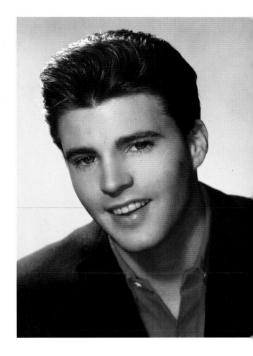

had gone from black and white to Technicolor." They took a cab to the Delmonico—no hotel in the United Kingdom was anywhere near the size of this skyscraper.

To Kramer's surprise, Ed Sullivan and his family lived in a flat in the Delmonico, and after Brian had discussed the Beatles' appearance with Sullivan, he and Billy moved to the Waldorf Astoria and met potential clients. "I fell in with the boy-next-door image of Ricky Nelson and Bobby Vee," admits Kramer, "and I think Brian had me there as insurance, just in case the Beatles failed." Brian met promoter Sid Bernstein, who was keen to present the Beatles in concert, and influential DJ Murray the K. Epstein felt that if they could conquer New York, the rest of the country would follow.

Brian was encouraged that British shows were doing well on Broadway—*Beyond the Fringe, Oliver!* with future Monkee Davy Jones as the Artful Dodger, and *Stop the World—I Want to Get Off* with Anthony Newley. The British films *Lawrence of Arabia* and *Tom Jones* were also doing good business, and the new-styled Carnaby Street fashions of Mary Quant and other British designers were starting to get noticed.

Opposite page: When Brian Epstein (center) first moved to London, he was living at the Grosvenor Hotel, in Park Lane. The Beatles performed there for a prestigious charity show on December 2, 1963, when this photograph—all looking unusually formal—was taken.

Above left: William Ashton, aka Billy J Kramer, was also signed by Brian Epstein. If the Beatles' revolution had never happened, Billy would have easily fitted in with the teen idols of the day: Bobby Vee and Ricky Nelson. He still had the hit records, but he seemed a throwback to the early 60s. In 2013 he released a new song, questioning why Brian Epstein wasn't in the Rock And Roll Hall Of Fame—good on you, Bill.

Above middle: Fantastic hair! Several of Bobby Vee's hit songs came from New York's Tin Pan Alley, the Brill Building—"Take Good Care Of My Baby" (1961) was by Gerry Goffin and Carole King. Starting in the 1980s, Bobby Vee had an impressive renaissance, topping oldies shows in the U.S. and UK, and working with his sons, the Vees. He has had to retire with the onset of Alzheimer's Disease.

Above right: Rock'n'roll fans are divided over Rick Nelson. Was he the last of the rock'n'roll stars or the first of the teen idols? He had a warm, sincere voice and his records were strengthened by James Burton's guitar and the Jordanaires' backing vocals. When the Beatles triumphed in the States, Nelson switched to country music and then formed the excellent Stone Canyon Band. In 1972, after performing on an oldies concert at Madison Square Garden, he wrote the bittersweet "Garden Party"—"If memories were all I sang, I'd sooner drive a truck."

continued on page 34

ECOUTEZ, VOULEZ-VOUS CONNAITRE UN SECRET?

Although it seems logical to assume that the initial reaction to the Beatles was the same in both the United States and Canada, this was not the case. There were different responses by marketing managers on each side of the border.

DURING THE 1950s, THERE WERE MANY BRITISH IMMIGRANTS TO CANADA. The Canadian Government offered financial help, and around 25 percent of all immigrants were British. Naturally, they brought with them their own culture, so there was a market for new releases from British artists. At the time there was not an impressive collection of Canadian artists to capture their attention.

RAY SONIN

IT'S YOUR OLD "CHINA" . . .

That's who it is . . . the voice from over 'ome. If you crave news and music from the Old Country, it's Ray Sonin's "Calling All Britons", Saturday afternoons from 4:05 to 5:50 with news, chitchat and "oojahkapivvy" as Ray so succinctly puts it. Sonin covers the broad vista of overseas news with breezy wit and all the comfort of the neighbourhood local.

YOU MEET THE NICEST PEOPLE ON

CFRB 1010

Ray Sonin, an editor of the United Kingdom's *New Musical Express*, better known as the *NME*, moved to Canada and in 1958 began a weekly radio show, *Calling All Britons*, on CFRB in Toronto. It featured "music and current events from the British Isles," and the show was on air every Saturday night until Sonin's death in 1991. Sonin would read out British news and play current releases. In December 1962 he read out a letter from a Canadian listener who had been to Liverpool and had brought back for him the Beatles' first Parlophone single, "Love Me Do."

Sonin is the first known person to broadcast a Beatles record in North America. However, in April 1962 the Canadian Decca label had issued "My Bonnie" and "The Saints" by Tony Sheridan and the Beat Brothers (that is, the Beatles).

Above: London born, but Toronto based, Ray Sonin was 56 when the Beatles came to North America. He had 100,000 listeners for his weekly show *Calling All Britons* on CFRB. The show was broadcast until he was 84, and he received an OBE (an award higher than the Beatles' MBE) for his achievements.

ONTO DAILY STAR

IN THIS SECTION: RADIO/TV/IN

CATTY, TORONTO, HAS HIS BEATLE WIG FITTED BY WIG SHOP MANAGER LEON COHEN
ce McLure eyes the male hair style made popular by "The Beatles," British singing sensations

BEATLE MADNESS INVADES METRO!

oronto's going mad over the Beatles.
A wig-making firm has sold 80 Beatle wigs in
past month and has a rush order for more to
the demand, says manager Leon
st customer here is Jerry Catty. The sheep-
style hairdo is admired by Janice McLure.
Two local radio stations—CKEY and CHUM—
ve pulled strings madly for tickets to Sunday's

Ed Sullivan show in New York, where the English
quartet makes its North American debut. It appears
CKEY will get the tickets, as prize for its current
contest.
The three guitarists and drummer have sold
millions of records in Britain, and are considered
the hottest popular entertainment property since
Elvis Presley.

Above: Like the U.S. papers, the *Toronto Daily Star* favors the Beatles' haircut as their distinguishing feature, not their musical ability.

Right: Al Boliska was the morning DJ at CHUM, and his newspaper column was lighthearted and carelessly written. The Beatles didn't wear corduroy and the quoted fee for the *Ed Sullivan* appearances is guesswork and overstated. He makes an intriguing comment on the allocation of tickets, though: certainly executives invited their families, but this didn't account for all the seats.

SATURDAY, FEBRUARY 8, 1964

Teens will flip wigs over $2.98 Beatle bobs

HERE'S
Al Boliska

Heard enough about the Beatles? No? Well, get this:

According to Dawn Hester, president of the Beatles Fan Club here, there are 13,000 members in Toronto. Dawn and Trudy Metcalfe, co-presidents, are going to New York this weekend on speculation. They have no tickets for the Ed Sullivan show tomorrow night, but they hope to talk their way in. Lotta luck.

Every available ticket for the Beatles' appearance on the Sullivan show has been grabbed by network executives and sponsors for their own teenagers. There were practically no tickets available hours after Sullivan first announced the Beatles would be on the show.

Those few who are willing to part with their tickets to the Beatles' appearance are getting up to $500 a pair!

More Beatle Bits: The Beatles this week have three in the top 10. This hasn't happened since Elvis Presley.

After their American appearance (Sullivan on Sunday live, and a concert at Carnegie Hall Wednesday), the Beatles go back to England to make a movie. They got their start in Liverpool.

Would you care to book the Beatles for a show? The Beatles' manager, Epstein, is asking upward of $20,000 per show.

Ed Sullivan reportedly is paying $100,000 for three shows, one live (Sunday) and two taped.

After The Star quoted me last week as saying that

the Beatles were good and wholesome but not all that different, I received many letters and was called many names by outraged Beatle fans. The one that tickled me most was the one that called me "an elderly fink."

CKEY is running a Meet-the-Beatles contest. Two youngsters fly to New York Sunday with J. P. Finnegan. The contest was announced Tuesday night and Wednesday morning's mail brought 3,000 entries. By Thursday morning, 10,000 letters had been received by the station.

Program director Gene Kirby tells me he received a call from the Beatles' manager in Liverpool many months ago. Epstein wanted to know why the Beatles' records weren't getting off the ground in Canada. In those days (early 1963) you could have booked the Beatles for peanuts.

In Canada the Beatles have sold 200,000 singles and 100,000 albums. This is very high for Canada where 50,000 singles make a smash hit. In the U.S., "I Want to Hold Your Hand" has sold 3,000,000 in a short time.

Paul White, national

sales promotion and advertising manager for Capitol Records (whew) says Beatles' wigs go on sale in record bars next week. They'll sell around $2.98.

Paul says hundreds of letters, addressed to the Beatles, are received by Capitol Records every day. Many are love letters to a quartet, others request intimate details about the boys. Most are forwarded to the Beatles.

A member of the British House of Commons publicly thanked the Beatles for saving the British corduroy industry. This division of Britain's textile industry had hit a real slump, but with the Beatles setting the pace with their corduroy outfits, business is booming again.

TRUE STORY: One of the biggest lines in "She Loves You," by the Beatles, is the "Yeah Yeah Yeah" which follows. At the Old Vic theatre in London last week a tense scene ended with an aged actor shouting "She loves you" and — you guessed it—a voice from the last row chirped back "yeah yeah yeah."

Phone Capitol records of Canada and you'll hear the switchboard girl chirp "Good morning . . . Capitol Records, home of the fabulous Beatles."

A new group in England call themselves the Ants. Other groups are the Grasshoppers and the Crickets.

Here's Boliska's choice of records this week—a country song: Miller's Cave, by Bobby Bare on RCA Victor.

It did not make any of the station playlists, and the single is so rare that a mint copy is worth several thousand dollars.

Although Capitol of Canada was owned by Capitol and, hence, EMI, it had a certain autonomy. A Londoner, Paul White, worked in the shipping department and became promotions manager in 1957. He decided which British and American tracks would be pressed and released in Canada. He could hardly go wrong with Frank Sinatra and Nat "King" Cole, but he also did well with Cliff Richard and Helen Shapiro. Many other British artists on other labels did well in Canada, and the Australian-born Rolf Harris was particularly popular, usually stopping at Vancouver on his journeys between Australia and the United Kingdom and enjoying success with the song, "Vancouver Town."

Because he came from the United Kingdom, White was more liberal in his approach than Capitol's Dave Dexter. Although U.S. record companies were not interested in "Love Me Do," Capitol of Canada took a different stance. Paul White authorized its release in February 1963 and publicized it in a Toronto newspaper. He followed it with "Please Please Me," "From Me to You," and "She Loves You." White did not, however, immediately release their first album. Following a listeners' vote, one Canadian station played Del Shannon's "From Me to You" in preference to the Beatles. Much to the annoyance of U.S. Capitol, import copies of "Roll Over Beethoven" made their national chart, and Alan Livingston told White that decisions as to what to release in Canada had to be approved by him.

The British music papers *New Musical Express* and *Melody Maker* were widely available in the larger Canadian cities, providing news of the Beatles to eager fans. There was no national music publication, but Paul White, who issued *Sizzle Sheets* for media and dealers, regularly featured the Beatles in his news. There was no national sales chart either, but when "Please Please Me" made the Top 40 on CFGP in Grand Prairie, Alberta, it was the first appearance on a chart by the Beatles in North America.

In November 1963 Capitol of Canada released the *With the Beatles* album in its entirety, but changed the title to *Beatlemania! With the Beatles*. This was commendably astute, as the phrase had been coined by the *Daily Mirror* in London only a few weeks earlier. The back cover included a dubious endorsement from the Queen Mother, saying that she found them "young, fresh and vital"—we do know that she had seen the band perform that very month at the Royal Command Performance. At that time the Beatles were better known in Canada than in the United States.

Beatles 1, 4, 8 in Top Ten

Here are the top ten on Toronto's Hit Parade:

1. She Loves You, The Beatles, on Capitol.
2. Anyone Who Had a Heart, Dionne Warwick on Barry.
3. Surfin' Bird, the Trashmen on Apex.
4. I Want to Hold Your Hand, The Beatles, on Capitol.
5. You Don't Own Me, Leslie Gore, on Mercury.
6. Um, Um, Um, Um, Um, Um, Major Lance, on Epic.
7. Big Town Boy, Shirley Matthews, on Tamarac,
8. Roll Over Beethoven, The Beatles, on Capitol.
9. California Sun, The Rivieras, on Delta.
10. Out of Limits, The Markettes, on Warner Bros.

Beatles swarm over New York

Lennon

McCartney

Harrison

Starr

BY ROLLIE HOCHSTEIN
Special to The Star

I've never seen a Beatle sing;
I've never even heard one.
But I will bet you anything
Their song is an absurd one.

NEW YORK—Not only had I never heard the Beatles, but I'd never heard of them till New York lost its head over their arrival here yesterday. I thought the locusts were coming. Or the Turnip Termites.

My 7½-year-old son, the authority, informed me that the Beatles are four rock 'n' rollers, real cool, from Liverpool. Their record, "I Want To Hold Your Hand," has sold well over a million copies since its release last Dec. 26. Their album, "Meet the Beatles," has passed 250,000 sales. They are coming to promote what apparently needs no promotion.

These Beatles, it turns out, sing in a bass-to-soprano range while they stamp about in collarless jackets and shaggy-dog hair-dos. They are England's answer to Elvis Presley, in quadruplicate.

When they perform, brigades of police must be on hand to pile the swooners in neat layers. They have given up one-night stands in Europe because those who can't get seats tend to riot in the streets. They are smuggled about in armored cars to protect them from their fans. Leaving Europe in ruins, they now essay their first visit to America.

They will sing, so to speak, on tomorrow night's Ed Sullivan show. They will give a mass press conference at the staid, old Plaza hotel, which they have chosen as their New York residence. On Tuesday, they will concertize at the Coliseum in Washington, D.C., and on Wednesday, they will present two concerts at staid old Carnegie Hall here, which may not survive the blow. Then they will do two more shows for the great stone face, the first attraction to appear on three successive Sullivan shows. Then, back to England for the first of three movies they are contracted to film for United Artists.

These are the facts. But the figures are fantastic. Sullivan's theatre seats 600. As of last Monday, there had been 50,000 ticket requests, most of them frenzied. Carnegie Hall seats 2,800. The concert was publicly announced a week ago last Sunday. Box office opened Monday and was sold out in six hours. Mike Merrick, publicist for Theatre Three, the concerts' sponsor, has been Beatle-infested.

"I'm getting calls from people I haven't been able to reach for 10 years!" he moans, citing a list of publishing potentates. "I don't mind dealing with legitimate people, gentlemen, they don't pull power. But I'm also hounded by all kinds of kooks, coming on like gangbusters. If they don't want tickets, they want interviews. I never saw anything like it I'm getting married this weekend and I don't even know who's got seats for the wedding!"

Theatre Three offered the Beatles a stunning $200,000 to do an extra afternoon show at Madison Square Garden. But so far, the Beatles' cool, young manager, one Brian Epstein, has refused—on the grounds that it might be nerve-wracking.

CBS has assigned a publicist exclusively to the Beatle problem. But all of the CBS pressmen are fending off ticket-seekers to Sullivan shows. Publicist George Ettinger, a man of calm efficiency, is admittedly harassed.

"Even Sullivan is calling me for tickets," he gasped.

Meggs Brown, publicist for Capitol Records, has been "in a meeting" for two weeks, while his desk is barraged with Beatling phone calls. And Budd Hellawell, their U.S. representative, has counted up to 50 calls an hour—ticket requests, interview requests, offers of concert bookings, requests from would-be manufacturers of Beatle dolls, packets, hats, shirts and even notebooks.

See BEATLES, page 28

Opposite page: Toronto's Top 10 shortly before the Beatles played *The Ed Sullivan Show*. It's still January and yet a surfing record is at Number 9: California dreamin' indeed!
Right: A typically sarcastic review of the Beatles from the older generation. Notice the pictures of the band: all of them captioned with the wrong name.

"We were let out of school early the day that Kennedy was shot," says Beatles fan Owen Coppin, "and I bought the album on the way home. There was nothing but news on the TV and so I played it all night, and I loved it."

"She Loves You" sold well in Canada through December 1963, Capitol finished the year with a single of "Roll Over Beethoven," and in January 1964 they released "I Want to Hold Your Hand." Then the Beatles' first UK album, *Please Please Me*, was released, with a few track changes, under the title *Twist and Shout*.

The Toronto CHUM (Top 50), and other charts, were indicative of how well the Beatles' records were selling in Canada before the group's American breakthrough. "She Loves You" debuted on December 2, and "Roll Over Beethoven" on the December 23. By December 20 "She Loves You" was at number 10 in the CKEY Toronto Top 40, and by the time of the U.S. debut of "I Want to Hold Your Hand", "She Loves You" and "Roll Over Beethoven" were number 1 and number 2 respectively on the CHUM Chart.

Nevertheless, *The Ed Sullivan Show* meant an even bigger boost for the Beatles in Canada, although by that time Beatlemania was well under way north of the border. "There were no fan magazines until after *Sullivan*," Owen Coppin recalls, "and I took some stills off the TV and sold copies at school. My brother had a darkroom, and we sold the copies for 10 cents each and made over $100. The girls were desperate to get anything."

Witnessing the Beatles' colossal success on the U.S. charts, Capitol of Canada quickly released singles of "All My Loving," "Twist and Shout," "Can't Buy Me Love," "Do You Want to Know a Secret," and the German-language "*Sie Liebt Dich*." On March 30, 1964, the CHUM Hit Parade in Toronto had seven Beatles titles in its Top 10.

TIME TO ROCK THE WORLD

Sid Bernstein had been reading the British newspapers and was intrigued by the success of the Beatles. It was reminiscent of the teenage bobby-soxers mobbing Frank Sinatra at the Paramount Theater in 1944. Bernstein booked the famous Carnegie Hall for two shows on February 12, Lincoln's birthday, a school holiday in New York. The venue was wary about staging pop music, given its prestigious history, but Bernstein told them it would promote "international understanding."

The music industry's trade paper *Billboard* covered what was happening on the music scene in other countries, so astute insiders would have seen that something was brewing in the United Kingdom. On the morning of November 22, CBS News broadcast a short feature about the rise of the Beatles—but it was quickly dropped in the light of other events of the day.

At half past noon, President Kennedy was assassinated in Dallas. The country was plunged into gloom. Then the Beatles shot to number one with the exuberant and life-affirming "I Want to Hold Your Hand." Although Kennedy's assassination may have had some effect on the Beatles' popularity—they offered welcome cheer—it was not a major factor. As George Harrison said, "There had been cover stories on European Beatlemania in *Life* and *Newsweek*, so it wasn't too difficult a job for Capitol to follow through—and the song itself was very catchy anyway."

Beatles chronicler Bruce Spizer also discounts the influence of the Kennedy effect. "It is there, but it has been exaggerated. It is hogwash to say the youth of America was despondent and needed the Beatles. For them this is over a month later, and life goes on. The Beatles was a fun story, and even if a reporter hated the band, he would have fun writing about it. The press gave the Beatles terrific coverage, and that helped fuel Beatlemania. Sure, the music cheered us up, but it was great music."

Walter Becker of Steely Dan says, "When I started becoming aware of music on the radio, it was already a pretty eclectic

Above: A DJ on a Washington radio station started playing a UK release of "I Want to Hold Your Hand" in December 1963, a month before Capitol's planned U.S. release date. The record caught on and spread to other cities, so Capitol's production team pulled out all the stops to get it into the record shops in under a fortnight.

Right: British policemen hold back Beatle fans who are queuing to buy tickets for a concert at the De Montford Hall, in Leicester. Notice that although screaming girls always made the headlines, there are more boys than girls in this photo—maybe they just pushed their way to the front of the crowd or maybe the girls sent their boyfriends to buy the tickets?

mix of Elvis, rockabilly, black New Orleans music, and other kinds of rhythm and blues records. There was some very poppy, fluffy stuff that was going on in the '50s and early '60s before the Beatles. When the Beatles came along, it was the perfect moment to rock the pop world, because there was nothing very substantial. Ray Charles did that country record, *Modern Sounds In Country And Western Music*, and redefined the genre, so there was interesting stuff that didn't fit, and some strange novelty records."

BREAKTHROUGH IN AMERICA

The CBS news item about the Beatles was revived by Walter Cronkite on December 10 when he was looking for a lighter story. He ran it at the end of the evening news, and a fifteen-year-old girl named Marsha Albert in Silver Spring, Maryland, saw it and wrote to WWDC in Washington, asking "Why can't we have music like that in America?" A DJ with the station, Carroll James, asked a flight attendant for the UK airline BOAC to bring over the Beatles' latest record from her next trip to the UK. She gave him "I Want to Hold Your Hand," which Capitol was going to release in mid-January. WWDC played it on December 17 and even had Marsha Albert introduce it. It was picked up in Chicago and St Louis, and all of a sudden three major American cities were playing a record that was not available. Capitol at first wanted to impose an injunction to stop them, but then realized they wanted stations to play their records. So they rush-released it for the day after Christmas. The kids had their holiday money, and suddenly "I Want to Hold Your Hand" was the number-one record in New York City—with the rest of the country following very quickly.

By the time the Beatles had finished eighteen days of concerts in Paris, "I Want to Hold Your Hand" was the number-one single in America, and they were set to appear on *The Ed Sullivan Show*. While in Paris, Brian Epstein met Norman Weiss of General Artist Corporation (GAC) who was in the French capital with his client, Trini Lopez. Weiss's associate, Sid Bernstein, had already booked Carnegie Hall to present the Beatles, and Weiss suggested an additional venue, the Washington Coliseum.

After the explosion of rock 'n' roll in the '50s, by 1963 the U.S. music scene had become staid. Robert Reynolds of the Mavericks says, "It was a special time in which popular music was still proving itself. There were people who thought it should just go away and that it was a passing fad. Just before the Beatles, rock was getting very lightweight, with the Italian New York or Philadelphia boy singers. They weren't very original, and they didn't have the talent anyway, although there were some good songs."

Opposite page: The Beatles had to end their set with a bow to the Queen Mother and Princess Margaret at the Royal Command Performance in London on November 4, 1963. John Lennon looks pleased with himself. The official star of the show was Marlene Dietrich, and when she first saw the crowds outside, she thought they were screaming for her.
Above: CBS news anchorman, Walter Cronkite, cuts an unlikely figure as a pop pioneer, but in mid-December 1963 he ran a news item on his nightly program detailing the rise of the Beatles in the United Kingdom. It was this short, light-entertainment piece that kick-started the radio airplay of "I Want to Hold Your Hand" and was a factor in the Beatles' breakthrough in the U.S..

Up until then, no British chart acts had had a run of hits in America. There had been occasional singular successes for Lonnie Donegan, Laurie London, Russ Hamilton (who was also from Liverpool), Acker Bilk, and the Tornados. Major British chart names, including Billy Fury and Marty Wilde, counted for nothing in the States. Cliff Richard's American tour had not established him. So the odds were against the Beatles. Another manager might have shrugged his shoulders and said, "Forget America."

2 THE FIRST AMERICAN VISIT

"Every radio station in New York was playing a Beatles record. It was absolute saturation."

GEORGE MARTIN

Left: The Beatles didn't know what reception to expect when they first stepped off the plane in New York, but the surprise was a good one: three thousand cheering fans came out to welcome them.

IN JANUARY 1964, THE BEATLES CAME FROM NOWHERE
to top the U.S. charts in three weeks. Tommy James, later the
leader of the Shondells, recalls, "I was fifteen years old, and
I worked in a record shop in Niles, Michigan, and Capitol
Records had a brilliant plan for introducing the group. In
December 1963, they put displays in American record stores
with the four of them turned around with their backs to you.
Each week, the record distributor would come in with a new
picture; it would fit in a tripod on the counter, and little by
little the group would turn around. The last one showed
you their album cover, *Meet the Beatles!* It was a brilliant
strategy, and things were at fever pitch by the time 'I Want to
Hold Your Hand' came out. Soon I was in a cover band with
patent leather shoes, and we wore Beatle wigs for our third
set, and the girls were screaming." (It should be noted that
this marketing device was probably a local initiative; there
is no evidence of an official Capitol campaign like this.)

The actor Billy Bob Thornton was always a free spirit.
"'I Want to Hold Your Hand' was the first 45 I ever bought,"
he says. "I worshipped Lennon, as many people did. If he'd
recited the phone book, I'd have listened. The Beatles got me

Far left: Thanks, John! The BEAtles flight bag was witty product placement for British European Airways—especially as they were flying Pan-Am on this trip.

Left: In many ways, the sideshow was as entertaining as the Beatles themselves. Here, a photographer tries to catch their attention, but it's unlikely to have worked. Anything other than a real moptop was never convincing.

Below: Cynics sometimes say that the reception for the Beatles when they arrived in New York on 7 February, 1964, was staged, but surely this gives the lie to that. Would a professional campaign have homemade banners with grammatical errors?

through my childhood. It was the world I disappeared into. When the Beatles came out, I was like, 'Okay, it's time to rebel against Dad. I'm going to be in a band.'"

It was not so much Lennon's rebellious spirit as the music for Jim McGuinn, later Roger McGuinn of the Byrds. "The very first Beatle song that caught my attention was 'I Want to Hold Your Hand.' I loved the bridge—the chords and the harmonies are just so amazing. The middle eight was a pop music invention, but the chords in that bridge are like folk music chords. People often pick *Rubber Soul* or *Sgt. Pepper*, but I would go for some of the first tracks: they are incredible."

As a result of Capitol's promotion, "I Want to Hold Your Hand" had sold over 1.5 million copies before the Beatles even landed in the States. Factories were manufacturing

Above: Proof that every newspaper wanted something on the Beatles' arrival in New York. Note that long hair, which seems perfectly acceptable now. It was long compared to American crewcuts, but the Rolling Stones and the Pretty Things were soon displaying even longer styles.

Beatle wigs, Beatle sweatshirts, Beatle hats, Beatle wallpaper, and, naturally, Beatle pillows. Nearly forty sacks of mail were waiting for the Beatles at the Plaza Hotel in New York when the band arrived to check in.

Their Pan-Am jet flight 101 landed at the newly renamed John F. Kennedy International Airport on February 7, 1964. It was cold and blustery, but three thousand screaming fans descended on the airport. They chanted "We Love You Beatles," an adaptation of "We Love You Conrad" from the Broadway musical *Bye Bye Birdie*.

Among the passengers were John's wife, Cynthia; press officer Tony Barrow; George Martin and his assistant and future wife, Judy Lockhart-Smith; London journalist Maureen Cleave; and George Harrison of the *Liverpool Echo*, taking advantage of sharing a name with a Beatle. The American record producer Phil Spector, returning from a visit to the UK, was on the plane, too. He hated flying but thought that travelling with the Beatles had to bring good fortune.

Granada TV, the UK television station that served Liverpool and the north-west, had not got the budget to send a crew, and asked the documentary makers, Albert and David Maysles to film the Beatles on their behalf. They were given extraordinary access to the group and *The Beatles—The First U.S. Visit* provides an insight into what it was like being a Beatle in the eye of the storm (although the answer seems to be constant smoking, joking, and mugging for the camera).

On arrival, the Beatles gave a press conference for two hundred journalists and TV reporters. Despite the number of people there, it was a surprisingly informal affair. Asked what he thought of Beethoven, Ringo quipped "Great, especially his poems." Another exchange went as follows:

Reporter: *Are you going to get a haircut at all?*
George: *I had one yesterday.*
Ringo: *That's no lie. It's the truth.*
Reporter: *I think he missed some.*
George: *No, he didn't, no.*
Ringo: *You should have seen him the day before.*

The jokes may seem feeble now, but everybody loved the Beatles' wacky humor, which was something new for celebrity interviews. They were giving daft answers to stupid questions and doing it in endearing Liverpool accents.

The band made as many column inches about their look as about their music. The *New York Herald Tribune* commented, "The Beatles hairstyle is a mop effect that covers the forehead, some of the ears and most of the back of the neck. The Beatles are all short, slight kids from Liverpool who wear four-button coats with stovepipe pants, ankle-high black boots with Cuban heels and have droll looks on their faces."

Above: Murray the K had effectively taken over from the disgraced pioneer, Alan Freed, creating his own madcap take on rock'n'roll at WINS in New York. But he was also a canny businessman and owned Portrait Music, which published many of Bobby Darin's compositions.

Most of the press were straight-laced newsmen, and radio DJ Murray the K (Murray Kaufman), of the station 1010 WINS, seized the moment with a chance to stand out from the throng. He pushed his way to the front and announced himself the Fifth Beatle. The Beatles joked about his straw hat, and all of a sudden he was in with the in crowd.

Impresario David Stein, who was to work with music promotor Sid Bernstein, says, "Murray the K was impish, and he knew he was onto a good thing. Murray butted in and took over the press conference. Some people couldn't understand him because he had his own language, Meusurray, where every word had an extra vowel or consonant. It was like Ebonics but very hip. He was Murray the K all day everyday but he was a very lovable man."

WATCHING THE BEATLES

The sheer impact of the Beatles on *The Ed Sullivan Show* is hard to appreciate today. Network coast-to-coast TV was restricted to three major companies—NBC, ABC, and CBS—and the Sullivan program was a prime-time favorite. As with Elvis in 1956, if they were going to grab America's attention, this was the way to do it.

"My father had a friend in England who told him about this new group who were making a big scene like Elvis. I saw an import of *With the Beatles* in a store, and I thought that they looked weird. They looked like beatniks with those turtleneck pullovers. Then they did *The Ed Sullivan Show*, and it was an epiphany. They looked great, and they were exuberant and funny and cute and yet tough at the same time. I don't know how they managed that. The girls wanted to rip their clothes off, and they were making tons of money, and I thought, 'I want that job.' From then on, I was a pop wannabe."

ANDREW GOLD (top)

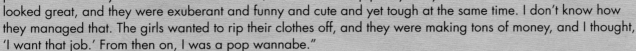

"Ed Sullivan said, 'Here they are, these four lads from Liverpool, the Beatles.' Paul McCartney stepped to the mic and sang 'Close your eyes . . . ' and the world exploded. The President had been assassinated a few months before, and so the Beatles couldn't have hit at a better time. They didn't sound or look like anything we had heard or seen before. On Monday in school I was in the cafeteria eating lunch, and the guy next to me was screaming in my ear about them. Everybody—the cooks, the janitors, the teachers, the police, every kid in school—was talking about the Beatles and talking at the top of their lungs. I've never seen anything like it."

GEORGE THOROGOOD

"When I saw the Beatles on *Ed Sullivan*, I realized that something different was going on here, and I wanted to start learning guitar. I learned those songs when I was ten or eleven. I know them inside and out. They are indelibly printed on my brain, however that works. It is always great to play those songs, as they are so much fun. What they did with harmony is fantastic. . . . They do 'This Boy' round one mike on *Ed Sullivan*, and it is spot on. Nowadays you can correct pitch and overdub and get it right, but that's what they sounded like naturally. Millions of people were watching them live, but they had an attitude and they were young enough to do it. They had guts."

JEFF ALAN ROSS, GUITARIST WITH PETER AND GORDON'S BAND

"I was with my parents watching *The Ed Sullivan Show* when the Beatles were announced. I remember the excitement, and I loved their sound and their looks. Everything about them was so different and so great—the Beatle boots and the haircuts. It was delightful, and—dig this, man—I asked my mother if I could join the Beatles fan club, as there was a kid selling memberships door to door. She said no, and I stole the money from her purse. I felt so

guilty about this that I never stole anything ever again. When the stuff started coming in the mail, I think she forgot that she had said no. I remember being in a friend's bedroom and on the wall he had all these cards that he had collected from chewing gum. I was envious of them, but I wondered, how much gum do you have to chew to get all of that? [laughs]"

JENNIFER BATTEN, GUITARIST FOR MICHAEL JACKSON

"I remember seeing the Beatles on *The Ed Sullivan Show*, which was our big variety show in the States. The hype was already there, of course, but they were great on the show, and they generated so much excitement. Like millions of other people, I was blown away and became a big fan. Although I wrote a song about John Lennon and his assassination, my favorite Beatle was Paul—great singer and great guitar-player too."

LOUDON WAINWRIGHT (right)

"I missed them on the first *Ed Sullivan Show*. The next day the kids were talking about nothing else. . . . I was cued in front of the television for the second appearance, and I was mesmerized by so much inspiration and energy from people so close to my own age."

RODNEY CROWELL

"I got my start by listening to the British Invasion, which inspired me to learn the guitar when I was about thirteen. There had been the Beach Boys before that, but it didn't really click with me until I heard the Beatles. We were talking about them all the time, on the bus to school, in the classes, and at lunchtime. Nobody talked about anything but watching the Beatles. They were bigger than Christmas. Ed Sullivan was very staid, like an undertaker, and these guys came across on the screen so vibrant, so that was a great juxtaposition, which helped them. They looked so different with their hairstyle, the clothing, and the boots: they could have dropped in from Mars."

MIKE BRUMM, OHIO EXPRESS

"I've been a Beatles fan since I was eight years old and they came over to do *The Ed Sullivan Show*. Everybody now is so busy ripping the Beatles off, and they're still great. Theirs are probably the records that I have listened to most over the years. They elevated pop music to an art form: no one took pop music seriously before them. People got really interested in everything about them, and that is because they were really, really, really good."

STEVE EARLE (right)

TAKING MANHATTAN

After the press conference, the Beatles were driven in individual Cadillacs to the Plaza Hotel next to Central Park. Huge crowds had gathered, and in their suite on the twelfth floor they watched the TV coverage of their arrival at the airport. The contrast with the staid BBC radio programming was immense: George Martin recalls, "I was astonished to find that every radio station in New York was playing a Beatles record. You could turn the dial and find a Beatles record being played. It was absolute saturation."

Phil Spector sent his act the Ronettes to meet them, and they wore their tightest, sexiest dresses. Ignoring his wife, John got Ronnie alone, but she protested that she was saving herself for Phil. John, not used to rejection, stormed out of the room, but he did call the next day to apologize. George

was having fun with another Ronette, Estelle, but felt himself coming down with an infection.

By Saturday morning George had developed a sore throat, and he stayed in bed while the other Beatles had a photo shoot in Central Park. Maureen Cleave told the London *Evening Standard*: "America gets madder, crazier, wilder about our Beatles every second. Coast to coast yesterday the news was 'Beatle has bug.' George's 'strep' throat came first: Cuba and Cyprus came after."

Francis Hall, the owner of the Rickenbacker guitar company, was delighted to see that John and George were using their guitars. He arranged a meeting with Brian Epstein, and he set up a display in a suite at the Savoy Hotel. The legendary Belgian musician Toots Thielemans was asked to demonstrate the equipment, although the Beatles were perfectly capable of playing the guitars themselves. John had bought his Rickenbacker after seeing Toots with one on the cover of a George Shearing LP. He said, "If it's good enough for George Shearing, it's good enough for me." On being shown Rickenbacker's new twelve-string guitar, John said, "I would like George to see this. Can you come back with us?" They walked across Central Park, followed by several hundred fans.

George perked up when he saw the guitar. He had played an acoustic twelve-string backstage with the Springfields, and he loved the sound. This was even better: an electric twelve-string. The ringing sound would be used by the Beatles, the Byrds, and the Searchers, and Brian arranged for a twelve-string to be sent to Gerry and the Pacemakers.

Left: Be, be, be my baby—Murray the K's dancing girls, the Ronettes, (from left to right) Estelle Bennett, Ronnie Bennett, and Nedra Talley. Ronnie was to marry the group's record producer, Phil Spector, who virtually kept her a prisoner in his mansion. In 1971 she recorded "Try Some Buy Some" for Apple, a song written by George and produced by both George and Phil Spector.
Opposite page: George was recovering from a sore throat and missed the band's promotional photo shoot in Central Park. It may have been a bleak day, but the three Beatles were clearly delighted to be in New York.

Vince Calandra, as well as their usual "stand-in," roadie Neil Aspinall, took George's place at a camera rehearsal for *The Ed Sullivan Show*, and Ed put on a Beatles' wig and said, "He'd better show up tomorrow or I'll be the fourth Beatle." He might have been the only Beatle, as they first had to be accepted for union membership.

Meanwhile, Brian had picked up a male prostitute and taken him back to the Plaza. A photographer seized the moment, climbing the fire escape, and taking pictures through the window. Totally embarrassed, Epstein had to confess to Capitol that he had been spotted. They traced the photographer and bought the negatives for $2,000. The photographer was instructed to forget about them, which turned out to be effective, as we still don't know who he was.

On Sunday morning, as they were driven from the Plaza to the theatre on West 53rd Street, the Beatles were amazed by the crowds. Fortunately, George's throat had improved, and he arrived to record what would be their third appearance on the show, but recorded first. George later recalled, "When they got a balance between the instruments and the vocals,

Above: A posed shot, but a funny one. Ed Sullivan was telling the three Beatles and Brian Epstein that he would stand in for George if he didn't recover in time for the recording.

they marked the boards by the controls and everyone broke for lunch. When we came back to tape the show, the cleaners had polished all the marks off the board."

The Ed Sullivan Show was normally broadcast from CBS's Studio 50 in Manhattan. The studio's audience capacity was 728, but over 50,000 fans had applied for tickets. Sullivan was cantankerous, not pleased with the hordes of screaming girls. He wrote his own introductory links, and while he was working on this, Brian Epstein said, "I would like to know the exact wording of your introduction for the boys." Sullivan grumpily replied, "And I would like for you to get lost."

Also making a guest appearance on the show was Olympic speed-skating champion Terry McDermott. When not skating, he earned his living as a barber, so Sullivan had him pretend to cut Paul's hair for a press photograph.

The Beatles opened with "All My Loving," "Till There Was You" (with a subtitle for John Lennon: "Sorry, girls, he's married") and "She Loves You," and they came back at the end with "I Saw Her Standing There" (the U.S. B-side of "I Want to Hold Your Hand") and "I Want to Hold Your Hand." The songs had been carefully chosen to avoid publicizing the Vee-Jay tracks.

Instrument manufacturers had a field day as the Beatles played their brands: Gretsch (Harrison), Hofner (McCartney), Rickenbacker (Lennon), and Ludwig (Ringo). Beat groups also wanted the same Vox amplifiers. The Beatles were unhappy with the balance and felt that John's voice was too low in the mix. Fortunately, they had been largely doing Paul's songs, and indeed, the casual viewer might have considered Paul the leader of the band.

The *Ed Sullivan Show* had a colossal audience of seventy-three million; youth crime hit a record low when the show was televised. Ed Sullivan later said that paying for the Beatles was the greatest investment in the history of American television. Sixty percent of all the TVs in the

Top: What's wrong with this picture? George was ill, so road manager Neil Aspinall stood in for him at a camera rehearsal for *The Ed Sullivan Show*. Sullivan decided that the huge Beatles backdrop was not needed, as everyone already knew who the Beatles were.

Above: Don't get too excited: Elvis and the Colonel (well, the Colonel really) often sent congratulatory telegrams like this one to other stars. Even if it wasn't as personal as it seems, it was still a nice gesture.

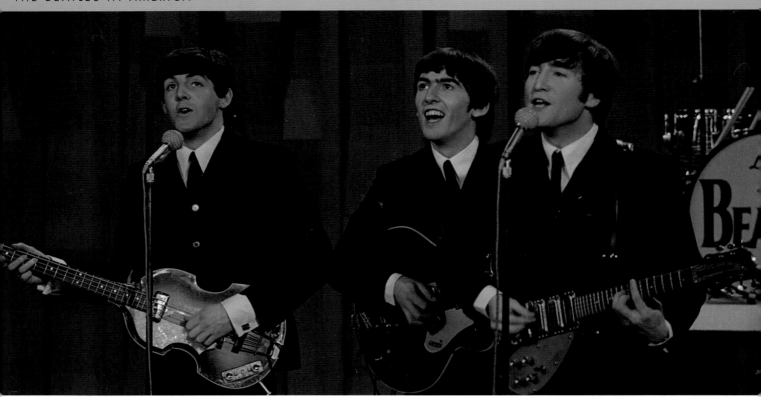

Above: Bill Bohnert's set design for the Beatles on *The Ed Sullivan Show* was simple, but effective. When you have a group that looks like that, what else do you need? A press release described Paul as the bouncy Beatle, George as the quiet Beatle, John as the sexy Beatle, and Ringo as the Beatle Beatle, whatever that might mean.

United States were tuned to the Beatles that night. Even the evangelist Billy Graham, who campaigned ardently against television broadcasting on Sundays, was watching. Graham said that the Beatles' performance displayed "all the symptoms of the uncertainty of the times and the confusion about us." (Smart of him to pick up on that.)

After the show, Murray the K took John, Paul, and Ringo to the Playboy Club, while George returned to his bed. Then Murray took them to the Peppermint Lounge, where Ringo was filmed twisting with the patrons.

The reviews for *The Ed Sullivan Show* were mostly very good. The *Washington Post* wrote: "They behaved in a more civilized manner than most of our own rock 'n' roll heroes. Except for the outrageous bath-mat coiffure, the four young men seemed downright conservative . . . asexual and homely." That's probably the first and only time that John was described as asexual.

The music critic of the *New York Times*, Theodore Strongin, wrote, "The Beatles have a tendency to build phrases around unresolved leading tones. This precipitates the ear into a false modal frame that temporarily turns the fifth of the scale into the tonic, momentarily suggesting the Mixolydian mode. But everything always ends as plain diatonic all the same." When shown this review, Ringo Starr commented, "Why couldn't he say whether he liked us or not?"

The next day the Beatles gave a round of press interviews and received awards in the Baroque Room and the Terrace Room at the Plaza Hotel. Once again, their banter mesmerized the journalists:

Reporter: *Who chooses your clothes?*
John: *We choose our own. Who chooses yours?*
Reporter: *My husband. Now tell me, are there are any subjects you prefer not to discuss?*
John: *Yes. Your husband.*

THE ED SULLIVAN SHOW

Above: Even in still photographs, Ed Sullivan looked awkward—as though he was wearing the coathanger as well as the suit. He didn't sing, dance, or tell jokes, but he got by because his Sunday evening show had an amazing array of celebrity guests. Nearly every big showbiz name from the 50s and 60s was on the show, though it was an ordeal, because the show was live and there was no lip-syncing.

Ed Sullivan, who was born in 1902, was a nationally known sportswriter who, in an unlikely move, became a gossip columnist. The syndicated columns under his name (though not necessarily written by him) appeared during the entire time that *The Ed Sullivan Show* was on air.

IN 1948 ED WAS THE HOST OF A NEW VARIETY SHOW, *Toast of the Town*, the debut of which featured the up-and-coming comedy/song duo Dean Martin and Jerry Lewis. From 1955 on the program was recast as *The Ed Sullivan Show*. Sullivan's UK agent, Peter Prichard, says: "Ed had seized the opportunity. When television came along, all the major film studios barred their artists from appearing on TV. They thought it would take away from the magic of the motion pictures. Ed became the only broadcaster they would trust, and he said, 'Look, it'll gain publicity for your movies.' The studios allowed Jimmy Stewart and John Wayne, who were big stars, to appear on TV, and to see them on [the small] screen was an extraordinary experience for the viewers. It worked well, and the rules were relaxed."

The Ed Sullivan Show was a variety show featuring singers, comedians, ventriloquists, jugglers, circus acts, and usually some culture—a snatch of opera or a scene from a Broadway play. Sullivan even had Albert Schweitzer playing the organ. But his most frequent guest was a mouse puppet, Topo Gigio. The whole family would sit down and watch the show, everyone knowing that if a particular act didn't excite them, the next one would probably be more to their liking.

When Ed was in his fifties, he wanted to associate himself with the new rock 'n' roll music, and after rival host Steve Allen had stolen a lead on him, he presented Elvis Presley—but with a gimmick. Elvis would be shown only from the waist up, as his gyrations might upset viewers. This could have been seen as ridiculous, but it was a masterstroke. Sullivan got sixty million viewers and at the end he added, somewhat paradoxically, "Let's have a big hand for a very nice person." He had given Elvis Presley America's seal of approval.

Other performers were less fortunate. When Bo Diddley was booked, Sullivan was aghast that somebody should be singing a song about himself, namely, "Bo Diddley." He told him to perform "Some Enchanted Evening" instead. Come show time, Sullivan introduced Bo Diddley, who pretended to go into a standard and then switched into the jungle rhythms of "Bo Diddley." Sullivan was furious and told Diddley that he would never appear again. Similarly, when the comedian Jackie Mason was cut short, he appeared to give Sullivan the finger and was banned from coming back. Bob Dylan never even made the show, walking out when told he couldn't perform "Talkin' John Birch Society Blues."

Sullivan was not a natural performer. He spoke with his chin tucked into his chest, as though he had no neck; and had a funny laugh. His strange pronunciation and botched introductions were a gift for impressionists, but Sullivan didn't mind; he even brought them onto the show. When the Italian tenor Sergio Franchi appeared, Sullivan said, "Okay, let's hear it for the Lord's Prayer."

His success, and that of his show, was based on his great instincts as a talent scout, even for acts that were not necessarily to his own personal taste. Would rock 'n' roll have made primetime TV without him? Would key black performers such as Duke Ellington and Ella Fitzgerald have had national exposure?

Above left and right: There was no entertainment show in America that came close to the popularity of *The Ed Sullivan Show*. Wooden he may have been, but he was a master at booking the right acts at the right time. Elvis Presley's performances are still regarded as classics today and very few of the major acts of the 50s and 60s did not appear on his show.
Opposite: It was a smart move to book the Beatles onto the show: their three appearances cemented the band into the American public's minds. When their first slot on the show was aired, the broadcast got sixty per cent of the viewing figures.

Ed Sullivan was benign and didn't criticize his guests, no matter what he thought of them, but he was uncomfortable with rock groups and often had backstage arguments. The Rolling Stones were told to sing a more chaste "Let's spend some time together" instead of the real title, "Let's Spend the Night Together." And after Jim Morrison ignored Sullivan's request to remove the line about getting high in "Light My Fire" (he claimed he got carried away), The Doors were not invited back.

The "rilly big shew" continued for 1,087 appearances, ending in June 1971. Sullivan died three years later. The studio premises remain today as the Ed Sullivan Theater; *Late Night with David Letterman* is presented there.

Left: Alan Livingston, President of Capitol Records, presented the Beatles with gold discs for "I Want To Hold Your Hand" and the *Meet The Beatles!* LP at the New York Plaza Hotel on February 10, 1964. For years, Capitol had resisted releasing EMI's British product, releasing only five of their records in 1962. By now, everything had changed, and telephone operators at Capitol were saying, "Hello, Capitol Records, home of the Beatles."

After the press interviews, the Beatles received gold discs from Alan Livingston for their Capitol releases. And in the evening, there was a cocktail party for the press, also held at the Plaza. The band had landed in America with a bang, but this was just the first leg of their visit.

Next stop was to be Washington, and a concert at the Coliseum. Planes were grounded because of overnight snow, and the Beatles had to travel by train. A special coach was added to the train exclusively for their use, which meant that the media (including Murray the K) had access to them for the whole journey.

The Beatles were intrigued with their first experience of eating hamburgers from a club car. George dressed up as a waiter while John and Paul parodied adverts they had seen on TV.

The Beatles were happy to visit the other carriages and mingle with the passengers, freely signing autographs and befriending young fans. The Maysles were still with the entourage and their film captures a delightful moment where Ringo talks to a young girl and answers her questions.

The train arrived at Union Station, where two thousand fans had braved a blizzard to welcome them. The Beatles were interviewed by Carroll James of WWDC, who had been one of the first U.S. DJs to play "I Want to Hold Your Hand" in December 1963. He was also to be the MC (Master of Ceremonies) for the evening. The Beatles stayed at the Shoreham Hotel, where they had booked the whole seventh floor, to ensure their privacy. One family had refused to budge, so the hotel cut off their hot water, electricity, and heat: hardly the right way for a reputable hotel to act.

Above: Outside the Washington Coliseum, the Beatles stage a snowball fight for the cameras. Note that McCartney is using his left hand: his left-handed bass was one of the distinctive characteristics of the Beatles.
Right: En route to Washington by train, the band and their entourage—including journalists and photographers—had a carriage to themselves, but they also mingled with ordinary passengers on the train without any of the usual fan problems.

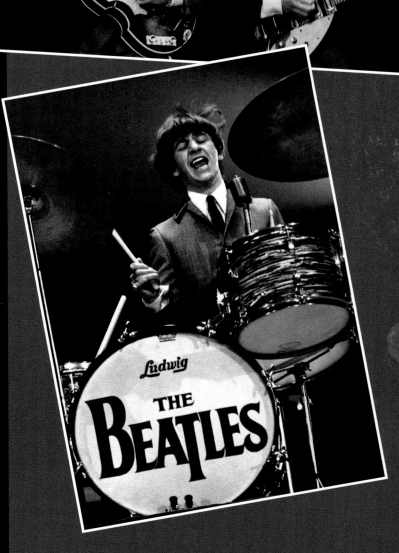

All photographs: The Beatles rose to every challenge that came their way. Their first stage appearance in the U.S. was at a large sports arena in Washington. They performed with the audience on all sides (main picture) and it didn't faze them at all: John and Paul (above right) look calm and relaxed. George Harrison (above) is captured in total ecstasy, and Ringo (right) is enjoying his moment in the spotlight with "I Wanna Be Your Man."

ON THE SCENE EXCLUSIVE

Photographed by United Press International Candid Camera Team.

THE **BEATLES** AT CARNEGIE HALL

THEATRE THREE PRODUCTIONS

THE FIRST NEW YORK APPEARANCE OF THE

BEATLES

CARNEGIE HALL WED. FEB. 12

Written by RALPH COSHAM in New York
Over 60 Illustrations   A Panther Pictorial   2/6

CARNEGIE HALL

It's probable that Carnegie Hall had no idea who the Beatles were when Sid Bernstein sneaked their booking into the main hall for February 12, 1964. It was for his new Theatre Three Productions, and at the same time he booked Shirley Bassey (February 15) and Tony Bennett (February 21). Bernstein was keen to have the maximum possible audience for the Beatles and, to this end, he arranged for two hundred people to sit behind the group on stage on rows of folding chairs. It's easy to envisage how this could have gone horribly wrong.

In December 1963, Capitol had recorded the Beach Boys live at the Civic Auditorium, Sacramento, and an anticipated similar album, *The Beatles Live at Carnegie Hall*, looked attractive. However, the recording could not take place, because Capitol had not secured the necessary permission from the American Federation of Musicians. The powerful label really should not have messed up something this fundamental: after all, they had done it before and had had huge success with the two albums comprising *Judy Garland at Carnegie Hall* in 1961, but—this time—it was not to be.

"The Beatles came to New York in February 1964 for *The Ed Sullivan Show* and two Carnegie Hall concerts," recalled Bernstein later on. "The concerts were sold out before they even set foot in America. Carnegie had never seen a gathering like it—all the noise and screaming—and they told me never to come back. I had to use other venues for a few years after that."

John Lennon was unimpressed: "Carnegie Hall was terrible. The acoustics were terrible, and they had all these people sitting on the stage with us, little

Rockefellers." Indeed—Happy Rockefeller, the wife of millionaire politician Nelson, had brought along their children. Photographs like the one on page 61 show the stage audience clearly. They might have seemed to have the best seats in the house, but the view would have been mostly a view of the band's backs and sitting behind the amps, as they were, they probably couldn't hear them properly either.

Opposite page: Carnegie Hall was refined and sedate (bottom), usually host to classical concerts and small, acoustic performances, but when the Beatles arrived they caused quite a stir. This UK fan publication (top) commemorated the event—one that the management was not keen to repeat.
Above: Someone may have come on the wrong night. More likely, she was a chaperone, though many parents would drop off their children and collect them after the show: a freedom that probably added to the volume of the screams.

TOPPING THE BILLBOARD HOT 100

In the U.S., the *Billboard Hot 100* was the main measure of success for a band. The chart took into account radio airplay as well as sales and—of course— everyone wanted to be on top.

CAPITOL'S FAILURE TO SPOT THE POTENTIAL OF THE BEATLES' FIRST SINGLES WORKED IN THE GROUP'S FAVOR, as the smaller labels that had released them saw this as an opportunity to jump on the Beatles bandwagon and have their own hit singles, rather than getting sidelined by the big boys.

In the normal course of events, two singles by the same artist are not released at the same time, as the label would not want artists to be competing with themselves. This hardly mattered with the Beatles, as all the fans wanted anything and everything they produced, and the various singles raced up the charts together. Things came to a head on April 4, 1964, when the Top 5 positions on the *Billboard Hot 100* were all held by the Beatles.

The Beatles' new Capitol single, "Can't Buy Me Love," had shot to number one in two weeks and would stay there for another four, while their previous single, "I Want to Hold Your Hand," was still number four despite a seven-week run at the top. Their Tollie single "Twist and Shout" was number two, where it remained for four weeks. The Beatles' previous number one; "She Loves You," on Swan, was still at number three and spent eleven weeks in the Top 10. "Please Please Me," on Vee-Jay, had been hanging around the Top 10 for six weeks, reaching an eventual high of number three.

It's fitting that the Top 10 in this particular week should include someone who in his heyday was as innovative and as influential as the Beatles. Admittedly, his peak of popularity was past, but Louis Armstrong's version of a Broadway tune, "Hello, Dolly!" could hardly have been catchier and became just as much a standard as any of the Beatles' records—indeed, it replaced "Can't Buy Me Love" at the top.

BILLBOARD HOT 100 APRIL 4TH 1964
Top Ten positions
1 Can't Buy Me Love The Beatles
2 Twist and Shout   The Beatles
3 She Loves You   The Beatles
4 I Want to Hold Your Hand
                     The Beatles
5 Please Please Me   The Beatles
6 Suspicion   Terry Stafford
7 Hello Dolly!   Louis Armstrong
8 Shoop Shoop Song   Betty Everett
9 My Heart Belongs To Only You
                     Bobby Vinton
10 Glad All Over   Dave Clark Five

Other Beatles entries:
31 I Saw Her Standing There
41 From Me To You
46 Do You Want To Know A Secret
58 All My Loving
65 You Can't Do That
68 Roll Over Beethoven
79 Thank You Girl

The Beatles were in the *Hot 100* with another seven sides: "I Saw Her Standing There" (Capitol B-side, 31), "From Me to You" (Vee-Jay B-side, 41), "Do You Want to Know a Secret" (new Vee-Jay single, 46), "All My Loving" (Capitol of Canada single, 58), "You Can't Do That" (B-side of "Can't Buy Me Love," 65), "Roll Over Beethoven" (another Capitol of Canada single, 68), and "Thank You Girl" (Vee-Jay B-side of "Do You Want to Know a Secret," 79). It might seem odd that an A-side and a B-side can be listed separately—after all, one could not be bought without the other—but this is because of the way the *Billboard* chart monitored store sales and airplay.

Also in the *Hot 100* were two Beatle-related records: "We Love You Beatles," by the Carefrees, and "A Letter to the Beatles," by Capitol artists the Four Preps, who had seen which way the wind was blowing and released an astute tribute.

There were four records by other British groups—"Glad All Over" (10) and "Bits and Pieces" (48) from the Dave Clark Five, "Needles and Pins" (15) from the Searchers, and "Hippy Hippy Shake" (24) from the Swinging Blue Jeans—an indication that the British Invasion (not just the Beatles Invasion) was well under way. An advert in the same *Billboard* for a single by Chad Stuart and Jeremy Clyde declared them to be "As English as a Cup of Tea," and soon they too had U.S. hit singles.

At top of the *Billboard Top 200 Albums* chart was *Meet the Beatles!*, the Capitol album that was largely derived from the United Kingdom's *With the Beatles*. It spent eleven weeks at the top. At number two was Vee-Jay's similarly titled *Introducing the Beatles*, a shortened version of the United Kingdom's *Please Please Me* LP. Considering the legal restraints on sales, it did well to spend nine weeks at number two. At number 77 was MGM's *The Beatles with Tony Sheridan and Guests*, which combined four Tony Sheridan tracks with two others by Sheridan and six by the Titans. At number 135 was a Vee-Jay rip-off, *Jolly What! The Beatles and Frank Ifield on Stage*.

There were two more British albums among the best sellers— the tribute to John F. Kennedy from the TV show *That Was The Week That Was*, and Anthony Newley's stage show *Stop the World—I Want to Get Off*.

Bob Dylan was making his presence felt with *The Times They Are A-Changin'* (22), while one place below him, Elvis hung on with a film soundtrack, *Fun In Acapulco*.

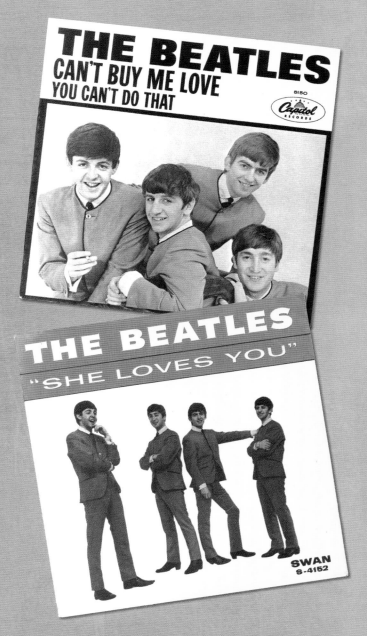

Above: Unlike the UK originals, the American singles came in attractive picture sleeves. These are very collectable, but it is hard to find sleeves in good condition today, as so often the imprint of the record inside is all too visible. Swan also released the German-language version of "She Loves You"—"Sie Liebt Dich"—as a U.S. single, both with the same English-language B-side, "I'll Get You".

Considering that most of the audience was quite young, it is surprising that Bernstein scheduled such late starts: the Beatles went on stage at 8:45p.m. and 11:15p.m. The bill included a folk band, the Briarwood Singers, and a tribute to the Beatles from various New York disc jockeys. A comic told a few blue jokes, and the program listed Paul McCartney as "John McCartney."

At least the MC, Murray the K, knew their names; he conducted a poll by asking the girls to scream for their favorite Beatle. Backstage, the Beatles were irritated by such inanity, especially when Ringo won by several decibels. They were tiring of Murray and his much-repeated catchphrase, "What's happening, baby?" The next day the *New York Times* commented that the Beatles had performed for three thousand shrieking Beatle fans as "inaudible accompanists."

George's sister, Louise, accompanied by Cynthia Lennon, had difficulty in returning to the Plaza. "Normally, we travelled in the same car as the Beatles, but they had their own limo that night. We sat on seats at the back of the stage, and at the end of the night we found that someone had commandeered our limo. We had no idea that we were so close to the hotel, so we took a taxi. Neither of us had any money, so we had to persuade the driver to take us to the hotel and then we went upstairs to get some."

After the success of Carnegie Hall, the promoter Sid Bernstein drove Brian Epstein to Madison Square Garden. "I knew the Garden wanted the Beatles. We could have had tickets printed within twenty-four hours and all sold within forty-eight hours. I offered him $25,000, but he said, 'Sid, let's save it for next time.'" As it happens, Sid's next plan was for Shea Stadium.

FLYING SOUTH TO MIAMI

Constantly on the move, the Beatles and some of their entourage flew to Miami, for relaxation and to prepare for the following Sunday's appearance on *The Ed Sullivan Show*. By mistake they had been booked into tourist class on the plane, but they didn't bother to change it.

Miami was inexperienced in handling large crowds of fans—and these fans pushed so hard against a plate-glass window that it fell onto the airfield. However, the city did provide a motorcycle escort for the Beatles' ride to the Deauville Hotel. John had a room with Cynthia; George, despite his hopes for his own room, was rooming with Murray the K (yes, he was still tagging along). Murray took them to see Hank Ballard at Miami's Peppermint Lounge. From the window of the hotel, the Beatles could see fans writing love letters in the sand. Lennon enjoyed playing his new Rickenbacker, which he used on the next *Ed Sullivan Show*.

On February 14, the Beatles spent time relaxing on a luxurious houseboat, the Southern Trail, owned by the businessman Bernard Castro. Of course, they were no ordinary tourists, taking in the local sights, and Miami police had assigned a personal bodyguard to the Beatles, Sgt. Buddy Bresner. They got along well together—so well that they even visited his wife and family at home one evening for a meal. They enjoyed sharing stories and opinions with a middle-class American family.

Right: From snow to sun in a matter of hours. Washington must have seemed a world away as the Beatles stepped out into the sunshine and warmth of Florida.

continued on page 71

SID BERNSTEIN

Promoter, agent, manager—Sid Bernstein helped to forge the careers of some of the best-known celebrities in America. He worked on hunches and instinct, but what an instinct.

AS A NOTED AMERICAN IMPRESARIO, primarily in New York, Sid Bernstein had huge success presenting an impressive list of show business greats including Judy Garland, Tony Bennett, and Elvis Presley—and the Beatles—and he made his own way into the business. Sid Bernstein never knew his parents, as he was adopted shortly after his birth in 1918 by two New York immigrants from Kiev—Israel and Ida Bernstein. One of his early memories was discovering Cushman's Bakery when he was seven; this developed into a lifelong passion for food. In later years, John Lennon would ask him for restaurant recommendations.

After his war service, Bernstein took employment with the booking agencies Shaw Artists and later General Artists Corporation (GAC), and he was responsible for booking major acts into Carnegie Hall, including Neil Diamond and Billy Joel. He presented Miles Davis for a week of concerts at the Apollo in Harlem, and he organized rock 'n' roll extravaganzas at the Brooklyn and New York Paramount Theaters with disc jockey Alan Freed. He defied Allen Klein, a notoriously tough negotiator, by refusing to give top billing to Klein's artist Sam Cooke.

In 1961, Bernstein took over the organization of the Newport Jazz Festival. Although it had been a success in earlier years, the residents of Rhode Island were tiring of this invasion of their privacy. To win them back over, Bernstein responded by adding two performances he was confident the locals would want to see—Bob Hope and Judy Garland.

Bernstein studied politics at the New School in Greenwich Village. A lecturer instructed the class to read a British newspaper each week to see how UK politics was reported. Bernstein became intrigued by the references to the Beatles, who were, at the time, taking the United Kingdom by storm. He had not heard their records, but his instinct told him to act. As GAC showed no interest in the Beatles, Bernstein contacted Brian Epstein himself and offered to present the Beatles at Carnegie Hall, though he had to work hard to persuade his backers and Carnegie Hall to take a chance on this unknown band.

"The thing you have to understand," said Bernstein, "is that the music business is not glamorous. Some performers may sing of love and beauty, but the business is very rough. I enjoyed knowing Brian Epstein because he had virtues that are not generally known in the business like elegance and loyalty. You could trust him and our agreements were done on the phone, without contracts. I like to think I borrowed from his technique."

Bernstein married the actress and singer Geraldine Gale in 1963; she was in the Broadway production of *The Sound of Music*, and Sid loved telling his friends "I married a nun." They had six children, all of whom helped Bernstein with his later productions.

Despite the many acts he promoted, it is the Beatles with whom he will be forever associated. In 1997 he was made a Cultural Ambassador for the city of Liverpool. His appointment was ideal as he was always singing the city's praises and as he says, "Liverpool made it possible for me to educate my children. I owe the Beatles; I own John Lennon; I owe Liverpool."

Above and top: Sid Bernstein presented the biggest rock concert to date when he promoted the Beatles at Shea Stadium in 1965, commemorated by this souvenir key fob. He then repeated the success following year. The 1965 Beatles at Shea Stadium concert set the template for other major rock concerts and it is regarded by many as the greatest of them all.
Opposite page: Bernstein is a huge man, who seems to exist on hamburgers and ice cream. He is also delightful company and a persuasive speaker, and in later years he became a favorite at Beatle conventions, where he signed copies of posters and spent many hours recalling events from his time with the band.

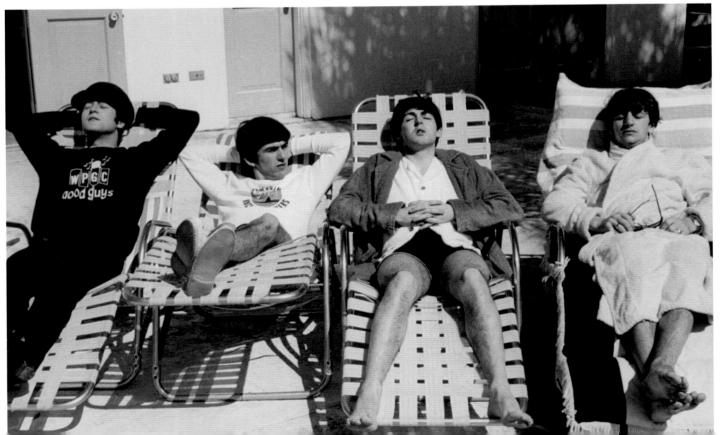

Later that same evening they attended a show at the Deauville featuring the comic Don Rickles. Rickles' stock-in-trade is insults, and he had some fun at their expense. A few days later, the Beatles had their first experience of an American drive-in movie theater, which was showing Elvis Presley's *Fun in Acapulco*—"Fun in Miami," more like: they were making the most of the opportunity for a holiday in the sun.

At a Miami press conference Ringo commented, "Everybody in Miami's got a pool, even if the sea is only a couple of yards away." A reporter asked if they would last as long as Frank Sinatra. "We should last longer," said Paul. "We don't drink."

On Sunday, February 16, 3,500 fans were allowed in for the rehearsal for *The Ed Sullivan Show* before seeing the actual show. The Beatles performed "She Loves You," "This Boy," "All My Loving," "I Saw Her Standing There" (with Paul's voice too low in the mix), "From Me to You," and "I Want to Hold Your Hand." Even though this was their second appearance and the curiosity value had gone, the viewing figure was still seventy million.

Boxing promoter Harold Conrad was a keen publicist, thinking of unlikely but effective events for his clients. The fight for

Thank you for your recent request for tickets to.. THE ED SULLIVAN SHOW FOR FEB. 16th
We appreciate your interest in this program and are sorry to tell you that it is not broadcast from New York City. We hope you will give us another chance sometime soon to entertain you and your friends at a program that does come from our New York studio.

Ticket Bureau, CBS Television Network
485 Madison Avenue, New York 22, New York

*THIS SHOW WILL BROADCAST FROM MIAMI, FLA.

Opposite top: The Beatles and Neil Aspinall relax in Florida, though John looks hot in his jeans, sweatshirt, and hat.
Opposite bottom: Sunbathing at the Deauville Hotel, John is still keeping it covered with his WPGC sweatshirt, promoting a Washington radio station.

Top: The Beatles spent an evening at home with their Miami bodyguard, Sgt Buddy Bresner (far right), and his family: it must have been a refreshing change, and the band regarded it as one of the most enjoyable aspects of the tour.
Above: Most *Ed Sullivan Shows* were recorded in New York, but many fans were disappointed when they applied for tickets to find that the February 16 recording with the Beatles was to be broadcast from Miami.

the world heavyweight title between Sonny Liston and Cassius Clay was taking place in Miami later that month. The public thought Liston was a thug, but they also thought Clay was a braggart. Conrad thought he could make Clay more lovable if he could present him with the Beatles. Brian Epstein was against a photo shoot, but the Beatles said, "No, we want to meet him; set it up."

Below: A terrific photograph of Cassius Clay (Muhammad Ali) with the Beatles: one out of a set of shots all full of fun and good humor. But did John Lennon really say, "You're not as stupid as you look."?

The Beatles went to Clay's gym and were mesmerized, as he was so well-built and good-looking (a rarity in boxing—a fighter can lose his looks very fast). Like them, Clay was a huge fan of Little Richard and Lloyd Price. There was a memorable photo session in which Clay lifted Ringo up and, as if he'd delivered a quadruple knockout, had them all flat on the floor.

The Beatles returned to England via New York and arrived in London at 8 a.m. on Saturday, February 22. Fans had camped out at the airport to greet them, and they welcomed them home from three

roof balconies. It was a shrewd move to separate fans from passengers, but there was chaos as many of the airport staff decided that they would rather see the Beatles than remain at their workstations and tend to their customers.

At a press conference, the Beatles were interviewed by David Coleman for the Saturday afternoon sports program *Grandstand*—hardly the program's usual kind of interviewees. George informed Coleman that Cassius Clay had said he would beat Sonny Liston in three rounds, to which John sang, "Liston, do you want to know a secret?" (Three days later, Clay—who later controversially changed his name to Muhammad Ali and refused to serve in Vietnam—knocked out Sonny Liston in Miami Beach in seven rounds: not as easy as the three that he predicted).

The following day, the Beatles were again seen on *The Ed Sullivan Show*. This was the performance that had been recorded first; they did "Twist and Shout," "Please Please Me," and "I Want to Hold Your Hand." It was another triumph. The Beatles remained loyal to Ed Sullivan, appearing again in August 1965 and also offering film clips in 1965, 1967, and 1970. Surprisingly, Ed Sullivan had had the Beatles on the show before their Capitol label mates, the Beach Boys, even though the California band had had hit singles since 1962.

Right: The Beatles had been in the U.S. for just two weeks, but by the time they returned home they were all over the covers of magazines and the papers. *Newsweek* of 24 February, 1964 (top right), devoted its entire cover to the band, while the *Saturday Evening Post*, 21 March, 1964, looked back over this first visit and promised a probing analysis of the band's "incredible power to evoke frenzied emotions among the young."

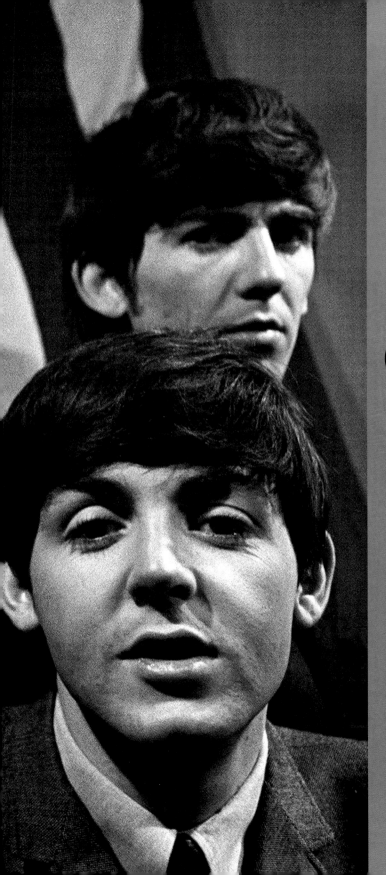

3 THE BRITISH INVASION

"We would take American songs like 'I'm Into Something Good' and 'Silhouettes' and add what we thought was enthusiasm, which meant doing it faster. You could call us the original punk band."

PETER NOONE, HERMAN'S HERMITS

Left: The Beatles posed in front of the Stars and Stripes for a photo shoot in April 1964, leading up to their first U.S. tour, but they were not the only British acts trying their luck in the American market.

IN 1775, DURING THE REVOLUTIONARY WAR, Paul Revere galloped through the countryside, warning everyone that "The British are coming!" The British returned in 1964, and this time they won a cultural revolution. So many British acts had followed the Beatles into the UK charts that it was inevitable that any new group would want success in the bigger and far more lucrative U.S. market.

As in the United Kingdom, the Beatles' biggest rivals were the Rolling Stones. Soon the Stones were touring and making network appearances. They had several U.S. hits that were not singles in the United Kingdom, including "Time Is On My Side" and "As Tears Go By." Their UK number one, "Little Red Rooster," was not even a U.S. single because it was considered too sleazy (and too bluesy) for daytime radio play, and when they wanted to perform "Let's Spend The Night Together" on *The Ed Sullivan Show*, Sullivan told them to sing "Let's Spend Some Time Together" instead.

Whereas the early '60s teen idols, both in Britain and America, had been good-looking, immaculately groomed youngsters, there were now the sullen, unkempt Rolling Stones and the belligerent Pretty Things, who were the antithesis of their name. Mick Jagger, Van Morrison (Them), Pete Townshend (the Who), and Ray Davies (the Kinks) hardly had the looks of poster boys.

The beat group members were, on the whole, a little older than the previous teen idols, and several had had further education, often at art college. When Mick Jagger was touring the United Kingdom with the Everly Brothers, he received a letter telling him either to return to the London School of Economics or leave. He left. Because of their education, they were able to think more creatively and often had a flair for design. Some of the best art of the '60s is on album covers, and the groups wore adventurous fashions—think of Pete Townshend and his Union Jack jacket.

MADE FOR AMERICA

But the Beatles, at least for 1964–65, had a cuteness that the Rolling Stones, the Who, or the Kinks never possessed, and this was especially significant in appealing to the preteen market. There were several bands that played on cuteness, but their music was largely ephemeral. The prime example is Herman's Hermits, with their cheeky, cherubic, and cheerful lead singer, Peter Noone. Their record producer, Mickie Most, thought that Noone would be perfect for America, as he resembled a young Kennedy. Herman's Hermits had ten hits in

Left: The Rolling Stones in New York, June 1964. Unlike the Beatles, they did not come to the U.S. with a hit record, but the tour went well and included two concerts at Carnegie Hall. The crowds outside were so fanatical that the Stones were ordered not to wave from the windows.
Right: George loved guitars. Even when he drew pictures, his favorite subject was always a guitar.

the United Kingdom—including a number one with their first record, "I'm Into Something Good," written by Gerry Goffin and Carole King—but they successfully released singles and albums in the United States in quick succession. Their U.S. number ones—"Mrs. Brown, You've Got a Lovely Daughter" and "I'm Henry the Eighth, I Am"—were not even singles in the United Kingdom; nor were their revival of George Formby's "Leaning on a Lamppost" and the Ray Davies *faux* music hall song "Dandy."

The New Vaudeville Band's "Winchester Cathedral," Peter and Gordon's "Lady Godiva," and the Small Faces' "Itchycoo Park" and "Lazy Sunday"—admittedly with psychedelic overtones—also fell into this new vaudeville area. Although

the retro sound often did well in the United Kingdom, the records usually fared better in the United States. Mickie Most didn't release UK singles of such songs by Herman's Hermits because he was mindful of what had happened to Lonnie Donegan—the skiffle star had fallen from grace because of a succession of music hall sing-alongs.

Although the Rolling Stones' geography is lamentable in "Route 66" (they didn't check on what they were supposed to be singing and their place names are all over the place), Jan and Dean were no more knowledgeable in "From All Over the World," in which they refer to "the Rolling Stones from Liverpool," and the Supremes released an album, *A Bit of Liverpool*, which included hits by the Animals and the Dave

Clark Five. The DC5 were branded as the Tottenham Sound in the UK, but that term meant nothing in America.

The Dave Clark Five's brash, unsubtle records were largely regarded with amusement in the UK, and the prominent saxophone sounded old-fashioned. They looked distinctive, if old-hat, in their dark jackets and white trousers, but Clark, a shrewd businessman, knew how to exploit the young American market, and they became a phenomenon, scoring eleven hit singles in a year. Their U.S. number one, a revival of Bobby Day's "Over and Over," was not released in the UK. Their other U.S. hits included "Glad All Over," "Bits and Pieces," and "Catch Us If You Can," as well as a UK B-side, the wistful ballad "Because," which reached number three.

Opposite page: The child is the father to the man. The Beatles enjoyed playing with model cars and John even took his Scalextric models on tour.

Above left: The youngest star of the British Invasion: Peter Noone, aka Herman, born November 5, 1947. His surname is pronounced "Noon," but you can imagine the trouble he had when plane seats were allocated to "No one."

Above right: The Dave Clark Five were led by their drummer, Dave Clark. The group had nothing like the Beatles' musical ability, but Clark was a brilliant entrepreneur, who skillfully took his group to the top.

continued on page 84

MAKING MUGS OF THE BEATLES

Beatles merchandise was a much bigger industry in the U.S. than in Britain, but the band found their names and faces on an array of products from hair brushes to bubble bath, and coin purses to candy—much of it totally unrelated to the music.

IT WASN'T UNTIL THE 1950s that the managers of American entertainers and movie stars realized that there were enormous spin-off benefits in merchandising, both financially and in name awareness. There had long been fan magazines; now there were posters, pens, lunchboxes, mugs, and all manner of other ephemera for die-hard fans to collect.

For years the Walt Disney Corporation had been very effective in finding ways to market its cartoon stars like Mickey Mouse and Donald Duck, and in 1955 there was a huge demand for coonskin caps and pocket knives following the Disney film *Davy Crockett: King of the Wild Frontier.*

The most successful marketing of a pop star prior to the '60s was undoubtedly that surrounding Elvis Presley; it has been said, though never proved, that his manager Colonel Tom Parker was responsible for both the widely sold "I love Elvis" badges and the "I hate Elvis" ones—all publicity is good publicity, it seems.

Back in 1963, the marketing of celebrities was in its infancy in the United Kingdom. Their biggest star was Cliff Richard, but

Opposite page: Some merchandise—such as this dreadful quartet—is so grotesque that you wonder how they passed any marketing quality criteria.
Right: The *Flip Your Wig* game took its inspiration from *Monopoly*. So long as you didn't open the packaging, almost any Beatle memorabilia will fetch a good price today.

outside of a few magazines and photographs, there was little for dedicated fans to purchase. So Brian Epstein's merchandising naïveté was understandable, as all this was new to him. In 1963 Epstein was constantly asked about marketing the Beatles, and he felt that it distracted from his prime task of managing them. On a low-key basis, he allowed his cousin to produce some items for the fan club. He approved the monthly fanzine *The Beatles Book*, and he gave the editor access to the Beatles for photographs.

Apart from these efforts, Epstein asked his lawyer, David Jacobs, to resolve the various issues. Epstein's main concerns were not financial; rather, he wanted to veto anything he disliked or thought inappropriate, and he determined that the Beatles would not officially endorse anything.

Although David Jacobs was a showbiz lawyer, he was over fifty and knew little about the marketing of pop groups. He knew a thirty-seven-year-old entrepreneur, Nicky Byrne, who had been a soldier, a club manager, and a racing driver, and he asked him to be involved. Byrne knew a good thing when he saw it. When he presented Jacobs with a draft contract, Jacobs asked why the commission had been left blank. Byrne suggested that Epstein should receive a 10-percent commission on all deals. This was ridiculously low, but Jacobs accepted the figure, and the contract was signed.

Nicky Byrne set up a company, Stramsact, to approve the merchandising rights; it had an American subsidiary, Seltaeb (Beatles spelt backwards). Byrne sensed that the main market would be in America: not only were there four times as many fans there, but they also had more money and were more conditioned to buy subsidiary products.

81

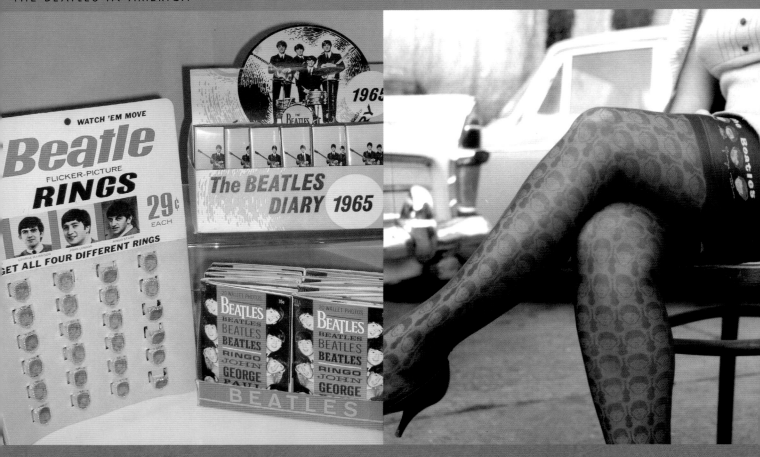

Above: Almost everything you can think of was Beatleized in the 1960s. Here we have rings and diaries, but unlike today there were no personalized T-shirts for individual gigs.
Above right: These would be highly prized memorabilia today—a pair of Beatles stockings.

Beatle wigs were a limited craze in the United Kingdom, as they were made of crude plastic, but the wigs really took off when manufactured by the Lowell toy company in New York, being far more lifelike and simulating real hair. This suggests that many U.S. fans took the Beatle wigs seriously and actually wore them—maybe when they were playing the *Flip Your Wig* board game?

The Reliant Shirt Company paid Byrne $48,000 for the right to manufacture Beatle T-shirts in the United States, and, with three factories working full-time, they sold over a million T-shirts in a week. You could wear the Official Beatles Bow-Tie for 49 cents—an unlikely homage, as the Beatles themselves only rarely wore evening dress.

The U.S. trade paper *Variety* noted, "Modern pop stars of the day represent a merchandising gold mine with royalties that can run into many thousands of dollars." In other words, astute managers could earn huge sums from merchandise, but perhaps Brian Epstein didn't read *Variety*.

When Byrne met Epstein in New York on February 7, 1964, he gave him a check for $9,700. At first, Epstein wondered if he had to deduct a commission, but then the realization hit home. If he'd gotten $10,000, then Byrne had made $100,000. Epstein couldn't tell the Beatles without jeopardizing their relationship. After all, John Lennon had told him, "You look after the percentages, Brian, and we'll look after the music." Capitol Records realized that Byrne had a gold mine and tried to bring it in-house by offering $500,000 for the company. The offer was rejected, and no wonder: this was a multimillion-dollar industry.

Epstein offered Byrne a place on his board, but Byrne knew he was already in the right place. Epstein insisted that the contract be renegotiated, and although his commission was raised to 46 percent later in 1964, the damage had been done. A legal

dispute dragged on for three years and during this time, some major retailers, including Woolworth's, did not want to enter the field, so the Beatles were not as comprehensively marketed as they could have been.

By the time the matter was resolved in 1967, the marketing peak had past. NEMS bought Byrne's company, and a new marketing company, Maximus, was established. The Beatles were never told where the money had gone, and after Brian Epstein's death in 1967, John told *Rolling Stone* that "Brian ripped us off." This was unfair, as Epstein hadn't profited from his misjudgment. Byrne, meanwhile, retired to his yacht in the Bahamas. He became exceptionally wealthy because of his connection to the Beatles, yet hardly anyone has heard of him.

In addition to official products, there were many unofficial ones, and many of the unlicensed products are now collectors' items. Today there is more marketing surrounding the Beatles than ever before, all of it strictly controlled by Apple.

Top: Two girls trying out Beatle wigs on a windy day in New York, February 6, 1964. Note the Gotham van: the Beatles would have thought of Batman.
Above: Much of the early promotion for the Beatles, such as this sticker produced by Capitol Records, was focused as much on their hairstyles as their music.

"The American market was different from the British one," comments Dave Clark, "and I recorded a lot of songs that were geared for that. 'Over and Over' sold three million copies, and it wasn't released in the UK. I just thought it wasn't right for the market. I could have been wrong. Unless you put the record out, how can you tell?"

The top three records for April 24, 1965, in the United States were all by Manchester bands: "Game of Love" (Wayne Fontana and the Mindbenders), "Mrs Brown, You've Got A Lovely Daughter" (Herman's Hermits), and "I'm Telling You Now" (Freddie and the Dreamers). Fontana, despite several British hits, could not repeat his U.S. success, although the Mindbenders without him climbed to number two with "A Groovy Kind of Love." The manic Freddie had a childish, repetitive dance that led to a U.S. hit with the cackling "Do the Freddie," a self-parody by an artist who was, himself, a parody in the first place.

Two duos, Peter and Gordon and Chad and Jeremy, both played the English card. Peter and Gordon were photographed in telephone boxes, and Chad and Jeremy wore bowler hats. Peter and Gordon's U.S. and UK chart successes were almost identical, although they released more albums in the United States, including *Peter and Gordon Play and Sing the Hits of Nashville, Tennessee*. Their rivals, Chad Stuart and Jeremy Clyde, had only one minor hit in the United Kingdom, "Yesterday's Gone," but had seven U.S. hits including "A Summer Song." The songwriters Roger Greenaway and Roger Cook formed the duo David and Jonathan, but their transatlantic success was with a song they didn't write: Lennon and McCartney's "Michelle."

Although they didn't succeed as performers, Greenaway and Cook wrote "You've Got Your Troubles," which the Fortunes performed so memorably with their counter-harmonies. Unit Four Plus Two appealed to a similar market, but their UK number one, "Concrete and Clay," only reached number twenty eight in the U.S. Although Joe Meek's production of "Telstar" had been a number one in 1962, little of his subsequent work broke through in America except "Have I the Right," by the Honeycombs, a good song inspired by Dave Clark's trademark thumping, with a girl drummer to boot.

Opposite page, top: Peter and Gordon. Peter Asher, the brother of Paul's girlfriend Jane, formed a duo with his schoolfriend Gordon Waller and they had hits with Lennon and McCartney compositions. Asher became a West Coast producer for such acts as Linda Ronstadt and James Taylor.
Below right: Chad (Stuart) and Jeremy (Clyde) were a folky duo marketed as another Peter and Gordon, but developed an originality of their own, especially with their concept album *Of Cabbages and Kings* (1967).

The northwest harmony bands the Hollies (Manchester) and the Searchers (Liverpool) deserved more acclaim in the United States. Starting in 1966, the Hollies had U.S. hits, but nothing like their UK success until their Creedence-styled "Long Cool Woman (In a Black Dress)" in 1972, which inexplicably reached only number thirty two in the United Kingdom. By then, their super-high harmony singer, Graham Nash, was one-third of Crosby, Stills, and Nash.

ONE-HIT WONDERS

The Searchers' UK hits included number ones with "Sweets for My Sweet," "Needles and Pins," and "Don't Throw Your Love Away," but their only U.S. Top 10 single was a chirpy revival of "Love Potion Number Nine," which bordered on novelty. Their stunning "When You Walk in the Room" deserved better than just the Top 40. Still, the Searchers are acknowledged as an influence on the Byrds, and Tom Petty, Richard Thompson, and Bruce Springsteen rate them highly.

The Swinging Blue Jeans had several UK hits, but only "Hippy Hippy Shake" made the U.S. Top 40. Similarly, the Nashville Teens found success only with "Tobacco Road," despite their rushing to Brooklyn to promote themselves with the help of Murray the K.

In 1965 the Kinks were blacklisted for refusing to pay union fees before appearing with Dick Clark on NBC. They were not allowed to perform in the United States for four years, and Ray Davies has called it "a plot to destroy us." This

THE BRITISH INVASION

For established American acts, already shaken by the dramatic impact of the Beatles, the British Invasion was like a warning that the end was nigh—and for many, it was.

"I had the number one record in America, with a sentimental ballad 'There! I've Said It Again,' and it was a historic moment when the Beatles replaced me with 'I Want to Hold Your Hand.' I was still number one on a radio station in Philadelphia and the Beatles were number two, but the Beatles had such hardcore fans that they were threatening the DJ. They said they would break his car window or flatten his tires. He said, 'Bobby, I'm sorry. You're outselling the Beatles here, but I'll have to drop you to number two.'"

BOBBY VINTON (Left)

"There was such an influx of British records after the Beatles made it that anyone with an English accent was in demand. It was absolutely essential that the disc-jockeys should be Beatle crazy and English mad. It made a major dent in the careers of so many American pop singers."

BOBBY VEE

"I left Columbia in '63, and after spending some time considering other record offers, I signed with Capitol. We spent two months getting the material together for an album, but before it came out, Capitol received the masters of some group from Liverpool. That was the Beatles. They started selling like crazy, and I was ignored. Capitol hardly had the capacity to cope with the phenomenal demand for Beatle records, let alone anybody else's. Consequently, I sat there for two years. I looked around for songs I'd like to record once I'd left the label."

FRANKIE LAINE

"The British Invasion had an effect on us. New acts were coming in and throwing rock 'n' roll back to us. You need new blood to grow, and that's what the British Invasion was all about. They were bringing new ideas to the party."

DION

"I didn't enjoy the tours, and I hated being public property. It is not very ego-satisfying to be screamed at by little girls and to be asked for autographs everywhere you go. I wanted to be appreciated for the music itself. Being famous in the '60s was a bit like being famous for being a newsreader. You are recognized everywhere, but all you do is read the news."

MANFRED MANN

"We were playing a big county fair in the States, and when we did 'Boom Boom,' I saw this big black gorilla coming at me, and he grabbed me round the waist and dragged me off stage, and the number ground to a halt, as nobody knew what was going on. It was this strange American idea of publicity. 'Ah, the Animals—get a gorilla!' Without telling us, the promoter had hired a giant of a bloke to come along in a gorilla suit and pull me off the stage. We were furious, because it wrecked the last number. He nearly crushed my ribs, too, and when I complained, he took his head off, and he said, 'Bugger off, go back to England.'"

JOHN STEEL, THE ANIMALS (In the pale shirt, above)

"We lost Graham Nash because he fell in love with America when we first went to America. I had met David Crosby and Stephen Stills in New York, and I introduced him to them, so going to America broke up the group and changed the course of popular music."

ALLAN CLARKE, THE HOLLIES

"We were asked to do a live LP while we were in Long Beach, California. They got everything lined up and tested the sound two days before. We went on stage to do the show, and we didn't realize that when there's thirty-five thousand kids screaming, you tend to play faster. All the tracks came out weird."

GERRY MARSDEN, GERRY AND THE PACEMAKERS (right)

"I do think that we made records that were perfect for their time. They are really good, and we would have been big anywhere. We were good on TV, and at first we didn't do anything controversial. I was too young to be cheating on anyone! Then we toured with the Who and got to know Keith Moon. This was our fourth tour and it was their first, and he hadn't heard of cherry bombs. He put one down the toilet and flushed and blew the pipe off the wall. Instead of telling the hotel what we had done, we ran away and hid. It got to be pretty hairy. I remember saying, 'I'm going to jump off the third floor into the pool' and then it was the fourth floor and then the fifth floor. We were just young boys on the road."

PETER NOONE, HERMAN'S HERMITS

"I've seen a reference to me in an American book which said that I was a pretty-faced crooner who sang nicey-nicey songs and was lucky to be buddies with the Beatles. That irritates me, because there was a different side to me. I recorded a very wild version of 'Sugar Babe' in California, with Mick Green on guitar."

BILLY J. KRAMER

"We made a live record at Long Beach, California, at the same time as Gerry and the Pacemakers. Gerry went on and got a terrific reaction, but the place went berserk when Billy came on. At one stage a policemen went over to Mick Green and said, 'Stop playing!' and he said, 'Why?' The policeman produced a gun and stuck it in Mick's ear. He said again, 'Stop playing,' so we did."

ROBIN MACDONALD, DAKOTAS (Billy J. Kramer's backing group)

"We went to America as the Merseybeats on a promotional trip. We played all around New York State for five days. We did seventy-two radio shows, seven television shows, and lots of personal appearances, and we aged three years in that time. We were shattered when we came back. The record wasn't a success, because instead of promoting one of our hit records, we went over with our latest single, 'Last Night,' which wasn't very good."

TONY CRANE, MERSEYBEATS

DOING IT FOR THE GIRLS

In view of her Beatles connections, if nothing else, you might have expected Cilla Black to have repeated her UK success across the Atlantic, but the magic did not extend to America. Her ten UK hits with two number ones ("Anyone Who Had a Heart" and "You're My World") was only transformed into a minor success with "You're My World." Burt Bacharach wrote, arranged, and conducted "Alfie" for her, but it was Cher and Dionne Warwick who had the U.S. chart success with the song (reaching number 32 and 15 in the charts respectively).

In terms of U.S. hit singles, the most successful British female singer was Petula Clark, whose UK hit records went back to the early 1950s. She maintained a bright, perky image and

Above: British fans were used to American stars saying, "Your policemen are wonderful," and now, in 1965, Cilla Black returns the favor. Despite UK success, Cilla had only one U.S. hit: "You're My World," July 1964.

Opposite: Petula Clark was keen to stress that she came from the UK. She made the best of the British Invasion with highy commercial songs from Tony Hatch. Prior to her song, the term "downtown" was not even used in the UK. Unexpectedly, she helped to promote racial harmony by holding hands with Harry Belafonte on a network TV show.

made some irresistible records, notably "Downtown," written and produced by Tony Hatch.

Of the other female singers (the so-called "dolly birds"), Sandie Shaw, a consistent UK hitmaker, found only moderate success in the United States, and Lulu did not break through until 1967. Marianne Faithfull, who became the female face of the '60s in Britain, could only manage four small U.S. hits. Dusty Springfield, the best soul singer that the United Kingdom has produced, had a succession of U.S. hit records and excelled with the landmark album, *Dusty in Memphis*, in 1968. But it wasn't a commercial success at the time, either in Britain or the U.S., Dusty herself didn't like it, and she did not have another hit for more than 20 years.

THE BRITS WHO DIDN'T MAKE IT

Apart from the Beatles, Brian Epstein's NEMS Enterprises had much success with other Liverpool acts in the United Kingdom, but none of them did especially well in America. Billy J. Kramer made the Top 10 only with "Little Children" and "Bad to Me," but the enduring memory of these is still enough for him to make a living on the U.S. oldies circuit. He should have done better, but a woeful performance on *The Ed Sullivan Show* did not help.

Gerry and the Pacemakers was the first act to reach the top of the charts with their first three singles in the United Kingdom. They didn't fare as well in the United States, but they had seven hits in all, including "Don't Let the Sun Catch You Crying" at number four and their hymn to Liverpool, "Ferry Cross the Mersey." Unfortunately, although Gerry had a cheeky, boy-next-door look, his Pacemakers resembled office workers and they just didn't have the appeal of the good-looking boys, the Beatles.

Some successful UK acts failed to make much impact in the United States—the old-stagers Cliff Richard and the Shadows were consistent UK hitmakers but only Cliff's revival of "It's All in the Game" made the U.S. Top 40 during the '60s. To everyone's surprise (including his own), the '50s hitmaker Adam Faith made the U.S. Top 40 with the raucous and atypical UK B-side "It's Alright," which owed its success to a powerful performance on the TV show *Shindig*, which was produced by a Brit, Jack Good.

AMERICAN FIGHTBACK

The American teen idols of the early '60s weren't going down without a fight. Both Bobby Rydell and Del Shannon recorded Lennon and McCartney songs, and Bobby Vee made a whole album in that vein. Growing your hair a couple of inches, wearing skinny trousers, and singing "yeah, yeah, yeah" was generally not enough, and some artists lacked the ambition and the talent to rework their acts. Ricky Nelson, Brenda Lee, and Conway Twitty found new careers in country music, and country star Roger Miller cleverly listed traditional attractions of Merrie Olde England in "England Swings."

"Trends change, of course," says rock 'n' roll guitarist Duane Eddy, "but I welcomed it, as I had been on the road for five years, only going home to make a new album, and I was tired. I was happy to sit in my home in Beverly Hills, and just go to the studio and cut a new album every few months."

A new crop of American bands—notably the Sir Douglas Quintet, the Lovin' Spoonful, and Paul Revere and the Raiders—found success through being modeled on British beat prototypes, and Roger McGuinn's vocals in the Byrds do at times sound suspiciously like John Lennon's.

For a short period, Liverpool and then London became the pop center of the universe, and some American performers, who had done little in the United States, established themselves in the United Kingdom. P. J. Proby's chart success started magnificently, but his wayward behavior led to him being abandoned by his associates and a marked deterioration in the quality of his music. With more effort, he could have captured the U.S. market and continued as a star in the United Kingdom, possibly rivaling Tom Jones, but such discipline was not in his nature. The Walker Brothers, produced by Johnny Franz, captured the cavernous sound of Phil Spector, but their lead singer, Scott Engel, was a complex, troubled individual not made for pop stardom. After playing in Little Richard's band, Jimi Hendrix was spotted by Chas Chandler of the Animals and brought to the United Kingdom, where he became a guitar superstar.

We don't know for sure whether any of the other British acts would have made the U.S. charts without the springboard of the Beatles' success. But their accomplishments paved the way for British acts like David Bowie, Elton John, Rod Stewart, and many more, in the '70s and beyond.

Above top: With their name, their suits, and their Beatle boots, those Tex-Mex boys, the Sir Douglas Quintet, did their best to look British. They didn't keep it up for long and Sahm (far right) became a pioneering figure in country rock.
Right: It wasn't hard to look ridiculous, but it was something the Beatles managed to avoid. As the name suggests, Paul Revere and the Raiders was part of the U.S. response to the British Invasion, but what other group wore tights? The vocalist Mark Lindsay is the one with the knobbly knees, and Paul Revere himself is on keyboards.

4 THE FIRST AMERICAN TOUR

Larry Kane: "What are your observations about the country of America?"

Paul McCartney: "We knew America was big, but traveling these ridiculous distances—well, it's fantastically big … I wasn't very impressed with American people until we got here, and I think they're great now!"

RADIO INTERVIEW, 1964

Left: Las Vegas in 1964 was seen as the home of the Rat Pack. It was very unusual for Vegas to stage teenage attractions, as the audience was too young to gamble, but the Beatles played there on the second date of their U.S. tour, in front of a huge American flag.

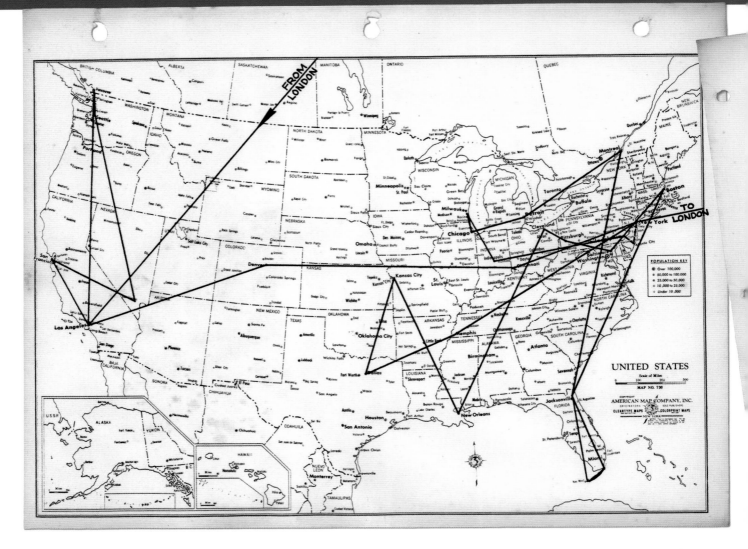

TO A CERTAIN EXTENT, ON THEIR FIRST NORTH AMERICAN TOUR the Beatles had it easy. Of course, they had the strain and stress of performing for twenty thousand fans in an arena, night after night, but by then the really hard work had already been done. The most complicated part was the planning. It was agreed that the Beatles would perform in the major cites of America and Canada; then the dates and fees had to be agreed, grouping venues to avoid zigzagging. Endless travel is exhausting, and even with optimum planning the tour had the Beatles traveling twenty-two thousand miles in a month.

The general strategy had the Beatles and their supporting acts playing the West Coast first and then moving to the east for a few days, going inland, and then east again, but there were long, grueling hauls such as from Montreal to Jacksonville, Florida, and then north again to Boston.

Once the schedule had been finalized, it was necessary to sort the transportation by plane and car, the hotels and accommodation for performers and crew, and the security. It was a logistical nightmare, and the organizers had to expect the unexpected. Promoter Norman Weiss likened it to planning the Normandy invasion.

A charter plane was hired from American Flyers for $38,000; the other performers would travel with the Beatles. These acts included the singer-songwriter Jackie DeShannon (who wrote "When You Walk in the Room" and was the first to

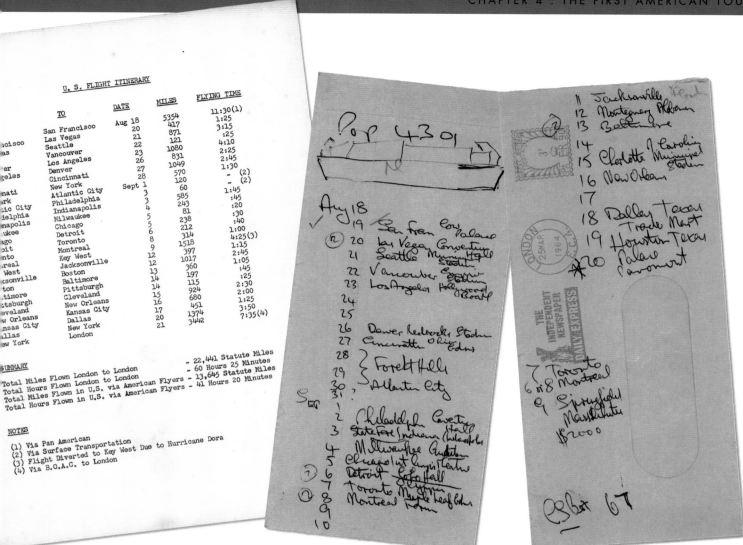

```
U. S. FLIGHT ITINERARY

                 TO              DATE      MILES    FLYING TIME
                                                    11:30(1)
         San Francisco      Aug 18       5354       1:25
         Las Vegas              20        417       3:15
         Seattle                21        871        :25
         Vancouver              22        121       4:10
         Los Angeles            23       1080       2:25
         Denver                 26        831       2:45
         Cincinnati             27       1049       1:30
         New York               28        570       -    (2)
         Atlantic City     Sept 1         120       -    (2)
         Philadelphia           3          60       1:45
         Indianapolis           3         585        :45
         Milwaukee              4         243        :20
         Chicago                5          81        :30
         Detroit                5         238        :40
         Toronto                6         212       1:00
         Montreal               8         314       4:25(3)
         Key West               9        1518       1:15
         Jacksonville          12         397       2:45
         Boston                12        1017       1:05
         Baltimore             13         360        :45
         Pittsburgh            14         197        :25
         Cleveland             14         115       2:30
         New Orleans           15         924       2:00
         Kansas City           16         680       1:25
         Dallas                17         451       3:50
         New York              20        1374       7:35(4)
         London                21        3442
```

```
SUMMARY

Total Miles Flown London to London              - 22,441 Statute Miles
Total Hours Flown London to London              - 60 Hours 25 Minutes
Total Miles Flown in U.S. via American Flyers    - 13,645 Statute Miles
Total Hours Flown in U.S. via American Flyers    - 41 Hours 20 Minutes
```

```
NOTES

(1) Via Pan American
(2) Via Surface Transportation
(3) Flight Diverted to Key West Due to Hurricane Dora
(4) Via B.O.A.C. to London
```

record "Needles and Pins"), the Righteous Brothers (doing okay, but yet to make "You've Lost That Lovin' Feelin'") and the Bill Black Combo (a saxophone-based instrumental unit, created by Elvis's original bass player, which had U.S. hits with "Smokie—Part 2" and "White Silver Sands"). In addition to opening the show, the Combo backed the other performers. Bill Black suffered from ill health and was not touring; years later, Paul McCartney was given Bill's original double bass by his wife Linda as a birthday present.

Also on the bill was a New York vocal group, the Exciters, who had a U.S. Top 10 hit with "Tell Him" and recorded the original version of "Do Wah Diddy Diddy."

Above and above left: Here you can see the distances the Beatles covered on their first U.S. tour. The proposed tour schedule in Brian's handwriting, scribbled on an envelope, came in for some late amendments. The Beatles never played Montgomery, Alabama, while Houston would have to wait for the following year. A gig was hastily added at Kansas City between New Orleans and Dallas. The map and list of flying times and distances were produced by American Flyers Airline Corp and given out at the end of the tour to everyone involved.

01 Cow Palace, San Francisco
Wednesday August 19, 1964
SHOWTIME 8 p.m.
ATTENDANCE 17,130 **CAPACITY** Sold out

02 Las Vegas Convention Center
Thursday August 20, 1964
SHOWTIME 4 p.m. and 9 p.m.
ATTENDANCE 8,408 each show, Sold out

03 Seattle Center Coliseum
Friday August 21, 1964
SHOWTIME 8 p.m.
ATTENDANCE 14,382 **CAPACITY** Sold out

04 Empire Stadium, Vancouver
Saturday August 22, 1964
SHOWTIME 8 p.m. (started 8:15 p.m.)
ATTENDANCE 20,621 **CAPACITY** Sold out

05 Hollywood Bowl, Los Angeles
Sunday August 23, 1964
SHOWTIME 8 p.m.
ATTENDANCE 17,256 **CAPACITY** Sold out

06 Red Rocks, Denver
Wednesday August 26, 1964
SHOWTIME 8 p.m.
ATTENDANCE 7,000 **CAPACITY** 9,450

07 Cincinnati Gardens
Thursday August 27, 1964
SHOWTIME 8 p.m.
ATTENDANCE 14,000 **CAPACITY** Oversold

08 Forest Hills, New York City
August 28 and 29, 1964
SHOWTIME 8 p.m.
ATTENDANCE 16,000 each night

09 Convention Hall, Atlantic City
Sunday August 30, 1964
SHOWTIME 8 p.m.
ATTENDANCE 18,000 **CAPACITY** Sold out

10 Convention Hall, Philadelphia
Wednesday September 2, 1964
SHOWTIME 8 p.m.
ATTENDANCE 13,000 **CAPACITY** Sold out

11 State Fair Coliseum, Indianapolis
Thursday September 3, 1964
SHOWTIME 4 p.m. and 8 p.m.
ATTENDANCE 12,413 / 16,924 (Sold out)

12 Milwaukee Arena
Friday September 4, 1964
SHOWTIME 7:30 p.m.
ATTENDANCE 11,500 **CAPACITY** Sold out

13 International Amphitheater,
Chicago, September 5, 1964
SHOWTIME 8:30 p.m.
ATTENDANCE 13,000 **CAPACITY** Sold out

14 Olympia Stadium, Detroit
Sunday September 6, 1964
SHOWTIME 2 p.m. and 6 p.m.
ATTENDANCE 15,000 each show, Sold out

15 Maple Leaf Gardens, Toronto
Monday September 7, 1964
SHOWTIME 4 p.m. and 10 p.m.
ATTENDANCE 17,766 each show, Sold out

16 Forum, Montreal
Tuesday September 8, 1964
SHOWTIME 4 p.m. and 8 p.m.
ATTENDANCE 9,500 and 11,500 (Sold out)

4 Vancouver

3 Seattle

THE BEATLES FIRST NORTH
AMERICAN TOUR
August 19 to September 20, 1964

6 Denver

1 San Francisco

2 Las Vegas

5 Los Angeles

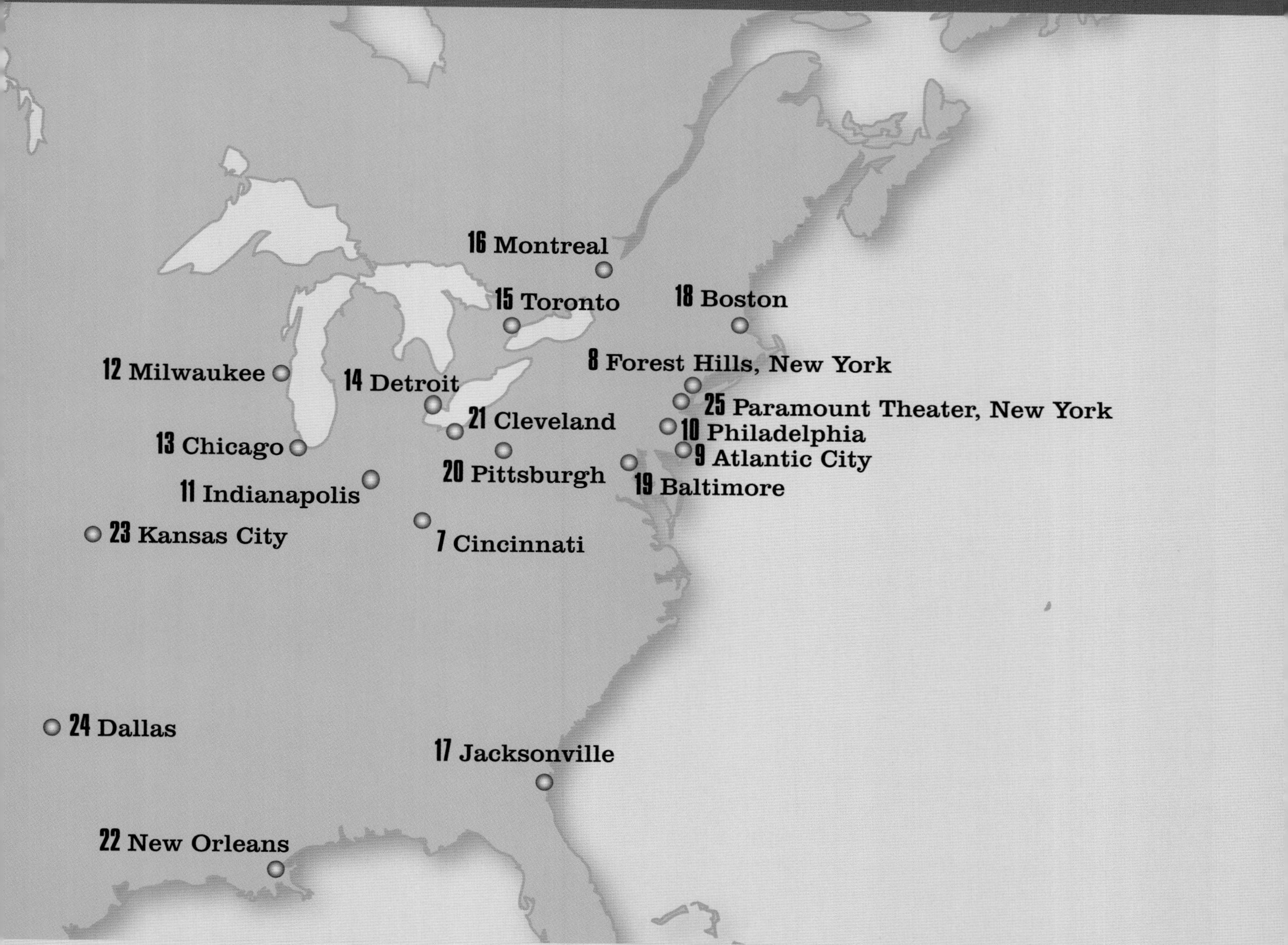

16 Montreal

15 Toronto

18 Boston

12 Milwaukee

14 Detroit

8 Forest Hills, New York

13 Chicago

21 Cleveland

25 Paramount Theater, New York

10 Philadelphia

9 Atlantic City

11 Indianapolis

20 Pittsburgh

19 Baltimore

23 Kansas City

7 Cincinnati

24 Dallas

17 Jacksonville

22 New Orleans

17 Gator Bowl, Jacksonville
Friday September 11, 1964

SHOWTIME 8 p.m.

ATTENDANCE 23,000, but all 32,000 sold

20 Civic Arena, Pittsburgh
Monday September 14, 1964

SHOWTIME 8 p.m.

ATTENDANCE 12,603

23 Municipal Stadium, Kansas City
Thursday September 17, 1964

SHOWTIME 8 p.m.

ATTENDANCE 20,820 CAPACITY 41,000

18 Boston Garden
Saturday September 12, 1964

SHOWTIME 8 p.m.

ATTENDANCE 13,909 CAPACITY Sold out

21 Public Auditorium, Cleveland
Tuesday September 15, 1964

SHOWTIME 8 p.m.

ATTENDANCE 11,000

24 Dallas Memorial Auditorium
Friday September 18, 1964

SHOWTIME 8 p.m.

ATTENDANCE 10,500

19 Civic Center, Baltimore
Sunday September 13, 1964

SHOWTIME 2:30 p.m. and 8 p.m.

ATTENDANCE 14,000 each show, Sold out

22 City Park Stadium, New Orleans
Wednesday September 16, 1964

SHOWTIME 9:30 p.m.

ATTENDANCE 12,000 CAPACITY Sold out

25 Paramount Theater, New York
Sunday September 20, 1964

SHOWTIME 8:30 p.m.

ATTENDANCE 3,682

The Exciters brought their own record player on the plane to pass the time between cities, and they interested the Beatles in B.B. King, James Brown, and Little Anthony and the Imperials. The mother of one Exciter, Brenda Reid, travelled with them, too: the Beatles called her Mama, and they loved the soul food she cooked.

Several hotels, fearing damage to the property, did not want the Beatles staying on their premises. Those who did accept bookings, having heard reports of foolhardy fans who would climb walls or go to other extremes to reach their idols, took out insurance against anything going wrong.

The American Federation of Musicians (AFM) was fiercely protective of its members' rights, as was the Musicians' Union in the United Kingdom, and in the past musicians had been allowed to perform in the other country only under a strict, man-for-man exchange agreement. The AFM's president, Herman Kenin, believed that permission had been given too readily to the Beatles for their first U.S. visit in February 1964. Presented with the application for the tour, he said, "We have a cultural exchange with other countries, but this is not culture. If they do get back into this country, they're going to have to leave their instruments at home, because there are enough musicians in the U.S., and too many of them are unemployed." In other words, the Beatles could perform only as a vocal group backed by American musicians. That would have been interesting! Kenin added, even more condescendingly, "We don't consider the Beatles unique. We can go to Yonkers or Tennessee and pick up kids who can do this kind of stuff."

The issues were resolved, and the Beatles played, but the FBI was intrigued by the AFM's stance. Although the Beatles were being promoted as a pop group, they undertook furtive inquiries to ascertain their political convictions. Could a pop group undermine a whole generation? Their notes for the first concert say, "Teenagers could be perfect vehicles for riots if racial elements or organizations, subversive or otherwise, decide to capitalize on this vehicle."

Left: The Exciters, who recorded the original versions of "Tell Him" and "Do Wah Diddy Diddy," were one of the tour's supporting acts.

Below: Fans in San Francisco scaled the outside of the Beatles' hotel by fire escape to try to locate the band's rooms. The tenacity of fans desperate to get close to their idols made many hotels reluctant to host the Beatles and the rest of their entourage, fearing damage to their property.

ARENA ROCK

The ease with which the Beatles made the shift from clubs to playing huge sporting arenas tends to be overlooked. At home on Merseyside, they had occasionally played to 3,500 fans in the Tower Ballroom, New Brighton; their biggest UK gigs had been up to 10,000 at the *New Musical Express'* Pollwinners Concerts. Now, between 7,000 and 14,000 was the norm; on the 1964 U.S. tour it would be 20,000.

The Beatles performed twelve songs in half an hour, sometimes speeding up or omitting a verse. For this, they earned an impressive $30,000 a day, but as we will see, it was dangerous work. Epstein was adamant that the fans should not be fleeced, so ticket prices were relatively low. They were

fleeced in another way, as the quality control was poor. It was rare for the Beatles to rehearse or even attend a sound check.

Although both "Please Please Me" and "Love Me Do" were U.S. Top 10 hits in 1964, the group did not perform them on this tour. With minor exceptions, they drew their set list from their big singles: "She Loves You," "I Want to Hold Your Hand," "Can't Buy Me Love," and "A Hard Day's Night," and two new songs, "You Can't Do That" and "Things We

Opposite: Many in the audiences of the Beatles' U.S. concerts were even younger than their British teenage fans. These girls in Las Vegas (top) and Seattle (bottom) seem overwhelmed by the emotion of the occasion.
Below: Fans would often grapple for squashed jelly beans from the stage as a concert souvenir, just to have something trodden on by a Beatle.

Said Today." George sang "Roll Over Beethoven," and Ringo nodded his head as he sang "Boys." They also performed "All My Loving," "I Saw Her Standing There," "Twist and Shout," and "Long Tall Sally." For Las Vegas they added "Till There Was You" and another new Lennon-McCartney song, "If I Fell," and for Kansas City, naturally, "Kansas City."

To give them their due, the Beatles always sounded happy to be there, but the screaming was as loud as the jet engines on the plane they had arrived in. The concerts were mayhem from start to finish, and Paul would encourage the fans to make as much noise as they could by clapping and stomping. In effect, they were developing stadium rock, although they didn't work the stage as today's performers do. Paul even shouted "Hello, San Francisco!" at the first gig.

In the United Kingdom, the audience was mostly in their late teens, but in America the Beatles fans were often preteens. The parents would usually drop them off at the venue, and the sheer youth of the audience led to additional problems of control. Most of them had never even been to a pop concert before. "Very young girls see the Beatles as cuddlesome pets," said Dr F.R.C. Casson, a London psychologist, "and when the pent-up emotion is released, it is almost impossible to bring it under control until its pressure has spent itself."

Back in 1963 George Harrison had said that he liked jelly babies, and the UK fans would throw the sweets at the Beatles as they performed. There was no such soft confection in America, and the U.S. fans assumed George meant hard-coated jelly beans. They would throw these at the Beatles, which could have caused injury. The police never frisked the fans for jelly beans, but they could well have considered doing so. At the end of the concerts, fans would take the squashed jelly beans from the stage as souvenirs.

Ringo, with his lovable persona, had become a firm favorite with the American fans. Part of this good feeling had developed when he was hospitalized with tonsillitis, and there was a spoof campaign, "Ringo for president," which held a mock convention in New York. The instrumental version of "This Boy" from *A Hard Day's Night*, was called "Ringo's Theme," and was released as a chart single. As Brian Epstein observed, "America discovered Ringo."

The Beatles did not meet many fans personally, but they met local fan club presidents at many of the venues. They appreciated how significant the clubs were to their popularity. But all four Beatles were uneasy when disabled fans were brought to meet them, as there seemed to be a feeling that the Beatles might actually have healing powers.

01 Cow Palace, San Francisco
Wednesday August 19, 1964

SHOWTIME 8 p.m.
ATTENDANCE 17,130 CAPACITY Sold out

With brief stops in Winnipeg and Los Angeles, the Beatles flew to San Francisco, arriving at 6:30 p.m. on August 18, 1964. Several thousand fans were waiting; a metal enclosure had been built for the Beatles, which had been named Beatlesville. In a perfect world, the limousine would drive into the enclosure and the Beatles would address the fans from a platform. But it wasn't a perfect world: the limousine pulled out just before the cage collapsed under the pressure of the fans, so the Beatles never appeared in Beatlesville.

The Beatles were taken to the fifteenth floor of the San Francisco Hilton, which was besieged by fans. Many had brought camping equipment to see them through a long vigil as they waited for a glimpse of the band. On the sixth floor, one female guest was robbed: her cries went unheeded, as the security force thought she was screaming for the Beatles.

John, Ringo, and press officer Derek Taylor escaped to Chinatown with Billy Preston, whom they'd met when they were playing with Little Richard in 1962. They drank with Dale Robertson, the western actor famed for the television series *Tales of Wells Fargo*. The bar closed at 2 a.m., and the barman ordered everyone out. Then everybody promptly went straight back in and continued drinking.

The Beatles were to play at Cow Palace. This was a giant indoor arena originally intended for livestock shows, but it also hosted professional sports events, the Grand National Rodeo, and was now being used for concerts, too.

Above: The Beatles starting their first concert, on their first American tour, at the Cow Palace in San Francisco, August 19, 1964.

Right: One of many such scenes at San Francisco airport, where fans surged forward to catch a glimpse of the arriving Beatles.

As the other acts performed, they had to struggle to be heard over the fans' shouts of "We want the Beatles!" When the Beatles did come on, opening with an intense and torrid "Twist and Shout," the police stopped the concert twice to tell the audience not to throw jelly beans at the stage. Many fans were injured, though not seriously, when they rushed forward. *The San Francisco Examiner* likened the sound to a "jet engine shrieking through a summer lightning storm." After their performance, the Beatles were taken to the airport in an ambulance—a useful ploy for escaping, until the fans got wise to it. Brian Epstein told the promoters of the remaining shows to step up security.

Below: The Sahara opened in 1952 and was one of the first casinos in Vegas to have a resident lounge act: Louis Prima and Keely Smith. *Ocean's Eleven*, the 1960 Rat Pack film with Frank Sinatra, Dean Martin, and Sammy Davis Jr was partly shot in the Sahara. Mostly, the hotel entertainment was middle of the road, but they booked the Beatles in 1964.

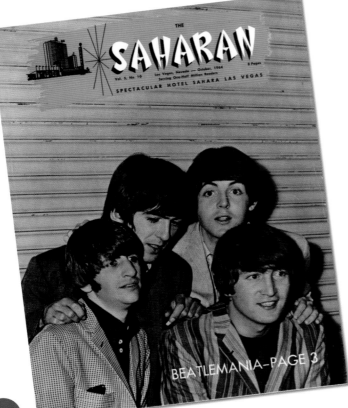

**02 Las Vegas Convention Center
Thursday August 20, 1964**

SHOWTIME 4 p.m. and 9 p.m.
ATTENDANCE 8,408 each show, Sold out

The flight to Las Vegas took only an hour, and the Beatles were taken to the Sahara Hotel. Although it was 1:30 a.m., and in those days Las Vegas had no resident population of note, the lobby was filled with Beatle fans. The Beatles settled into their suite on the twenty-third floor of the hotel's Alexandria Tower. The Beatles had been warned that America was a litigious society and that would-be fans might place themselves in compromising positions in order to obtain out-of-court settlements. Even the suggestion of impropriety could lead to a big payout, so the boys would have to behave.

Several fans had broken through the cordon and introduced themselves to the Beatles—in particular, twin girls, about fourteen years old, who settled down on the spare bed in John Lennon's room. John signed some autographs, and roadies Mal and Neil, plus PR man Derek Taylor, wondered how best to resolve the situation, especially as the girls' mother was in the lobby asking where they were. The respectable-looking journalist Larry Kane was dragooned to talk to her. Then a policeman brought down her daughters. Both appeared to be well, and they were happy at having met John, but it could have been damaging. John later said to Larry Kane, "Thanks, Larry. It was nothing, you know. Just some sweet kids."

The Beatles were instructed not to go into the casino because juveniles might follow. Instead, slot machines were taken to their suite. They came down at 2:30 p.m. for a sound check in the Convention Center, next door to the hotel, and they performed the 4:00 p.m. show against a backdrop of the U.S. flag. Although the official capacity was 7,000, the management let in another 1,408, some standing and some sitting behind the Beatles. There was a huge chant of "Ringo for president" in the buildup to the Beatles set.

The king of Las Vegas, Liberace, spent some time with the Beatles between shows, and George Harrison noted that

Pat Boone had brought his daughters to the show: "I think the first four rows were filled up by Pat Boone and his daughters. He seemed to have hundreds of them." He had four. Pat Boone recalls the concert, "I have never seen anything like the audience reaction for the Beatles. The fans would shriek from the moment they came on until long after they'd gone, and you couldn't hear them perform. It was somewhat like that with Elvis and somewhat like that with me, but with us the screaming was at the beginning, at the start of a song they'd recognize, then they'd go quiet, because they wanted to hear it, and go crazy at the end."

There was a bomb threat before the second show, but the police decided it would be better if the concert went ahead, as there could be violence from disappointed fans if it were cancelled. It went ahead without trouble.

Paul was uncomfortable with the news that the authorities at Jacksonville—coming up towards the end of the tour—had ordered the seating to be organized by race. He said that the Beatles would not play to a segregated audience and that "You can't treat people like animals."

Above left: Turn right, but if you go too far you're in the desert …
Above top: All that way to play slot machines. As the comedian Jackie Mason says, "Why do people go to Las Vegas knowing they will lose money?"
Right: Three front page news stories; three photographs: wherever the Beatles went, they were the only show in town.
Overleaf: Security forces in front of the stage protect the Beatles during their Las Vegas concert. From behind the band you can see the sheer size of the venue.

03 **Seattle Center Coliseum**
Friday August 21, 1964

SHOWTIME 8 p.m.

ATTENDANCE 14,382 **CAPACITY** Sold out

The Beatles travelled in daylight on Friday 21 August to Sea-Tac (Seattle-Tacoma) Airport, and the security was tight; fans were kept on a hill half a mile away. The Edgewater Hotel on Elliott Bay had erected wooden barriers and had the harbor patrol on the water. The Beatles had a suite on the second floor and were able to go fishing of sorts (at least for a novel photo opportunity) by holding rods out of the hotel window and dangling lines into the water.

Before the concert, a fan climbed onto an air vent by the stage and lost her footing, falling twenty-five feet to land in front of Ringo. Ringo rushed to her assistance, but she ran back into the crowd. She could have been killed—especially if she had landed on the drums.

After the show, the Beatles left by ambulance again, using their limousine as a decoy to distract the crowds. The roof of the limousine was wrecked by fans who thought the Beatles were inside. After the Beatles' stay in the city, MacDougall's department store purchased the carpet from the hotel and sold it in small squares as souvenirs.

Below: The Beatles fishing from their hotel window at the aptly named Edgewater Inn, August 21, 1964.

04 Empire Stadium, Vancouver
Saturday August 22, 1964

SHOWTIME 8 p.m. (started 8:15 p.m.)

ATTENDANCE 20,621 **CAPACITY** Sold out

The frenzied buildup to the Vancouver gig, the Beatles' first
Canadian concert, made the police realize that this was going
to be more than just a repetition of the hysteria they had
dealt with at an Elvis Presley concert in 1957. The Hotel
Georgia, fearing the worst, boarded up all their entrances but
the main one. The Beatles never got there, but a fake Ringo
did. A Canadian DJ, Red Robinson, hired a Ringo lookalike
to ride around the city. Ringo's ringer was mobbed outside

Below: A fan is overcome with emotion in Vancouver,
22 August, 1964. There are recordings of both Elvis Presley
in 1957 and the Beatles in Vancouver seven years later,
here in 1964. The fans are noisy for Elvis, but are mostly
shouting "We want Elvis!" For the Beatles, the fans are nearly
all girls and they are screaming loudly throughout.

the hotel, and in the scuffle that ensued around "Ringo's" arrival, a car ran over a policeman's foot.

The band's chartered plane took off from Seattle for Vancouver but had not gotten the right paperwork and had to return to resolve the issue. At a brief press conference, John Lennon explained the delay: "We had to be deloused." Asked about the most unusual request he had had from a fan, John, with a lascivious look on his face, said, "I wouldn't like to say"—certainly not the most tactful answer.

The Beatles had arrived later than expected, and when Brian Epstein saw the huge crowds lining the route, he took them straight to the football stadium. Although the stadium was full, there were fans outside trying to break down the gates, and the police set dogs on them.

The Beatles performed their songs quickly, ignoring introductions and stumbling over the lyrics of "She Loves You." They had fun in "Boys," as John and Paul sang "Be Bop A Lula" behind Ringo's lead vocal. They did not perform

"I Want to Hold Your Hand," and at the end, George shouted, "Run for your life" and rushed off stage with his guitar. One hundred thirty-five fans were injured, and many more fainted.

As the motorcade left, someone threw a bicycle in front of a motorcycle, and it was only by luck that an accident was avoided. The Toronto police issued a statement that all police leave had been cancelled for the Beatles' forthcoming appearance. One newspaperman, Jack Wasserman, reported that he was glad to get out of the stadium uninjured. When the fearless reporter returned a few days later for a circus, an ostrich sat on him and dislocated his shoulder.

The Beatles flew directly to Los Angeles, in high spirits after the charged concert, having both a pillow fight and food fight during the journey. They arrived in Los Angeles at 4 a.m.

continued on page 120

Below: The Beatles were well protected. In Vancouver, the troubles came in the venue and during their journey back to the airport.

KEY CONCERT: THE HOLLYWOOD BOWL

05 Hollywood Bowl, Los Angeles
Sunday August 23, 1964

SHOWTIME 8 p.m.

ATTENDANCE 17,256 **CAPACITY** Sold out

For one night only! The Beatles came to Hollywood for a sell-out, open-air concert. The next day they partied with Hollywood Royalty—although they were the stars of the show.

BOB EUBANKS, A KRLA DJ AND NIGHTCLUB OWNER, wanted to present the Beatles at the prestigious Hollywood Bowl. It was only the second concert he had promoted, the first being the instrumental band the Champs in 1959. Brian Epstein requested $25,000 in advance plus 60 percent of the gross receipts after the show. This was higher than the usual deal, and Eubanks really should have negotiated better. At a press conference at Eubanks' Cinnamon Cinder nightclub, the Beatles received four gold discs, and Ringo was given a giant key to California.

The Hollywood Bowl was an outdoor venue shaped, as its name implies, like a giant bowl. The concert took place under the stars, and the sound was clearer than usual. The security was more relaxed, as the stage was separated from the audience by a pool of water. And there was far less screaming, as many adults were in the audience. As a result, the Beatles gave one of their best performances of the tour. Even John Lennon commented, "It was the one we enjoyed the most."

George Martin had flown to Hollywood to supervise recording of a live album with Capitol's Voyle Gilmore. The Beatles were unhappy about this, feeling that fans were being ripped off, and the tapes were not officially released until May 1977. Two songs were screened on *The Ed Sullivan Show*. The towels that the Beatles had used to mop their brows during the concert were cut into small pieces and then sold to the fans.

The Ambassador Hotel, fearing trouble, cancelled the band's reservations, so they stayed at a Bel Air bungalow owned by British actor Reginald Owen. At a reception after the show, Long John Wade, one of two DJs who accompanied the tour, asked for the name of a girl lounging on a sofa bed with John Lennon. Lennon hit Wade, but quickly made it up with him.

The next day saw an ice cream party held as a fundraiser to benefit the Hemophilia Foundation, and organized by Capitol executive Alan Livingston. The Beatles, perched on bar stools under the trees, met Hollywood superstars Edward G. Robinson, Jack Palance, Lucille Ball, Peter Sellers, Nancy Sinatra, and Doris Day, as well as gossip columnist Hedda Hopper. Lloyd Bridges brought along his fourteen-year-old son Jeff. "It was harder than playing," said John. "You've got to sit on a stool and meet three hundred people of all ages."

The blonde sex bomb Jayne Mansfield wanted to meet the Beatles one-on-one (or rather, John-on-one) and suggested the Whisky-a-Go-Go on Sunset Strip, where Johnny Rivers was performing. John went, along with George and Ringo. George threw Coca-Cola over a photographer who got too close, and it splashed onto another blonde bombshell, Mamie Van Doren. George wrote home, "You can see why we don't usually bother going out now, because it's no fun, and soft gits like Mansfield try and get a bit of publicity out of us." John seemed to disagree, as he and Jayne left the club hand in hand.

Later in the evening the Beatles were invited to Burt Lancaster's home, where they watched the Pink Panther movie *A Shot in the Dark*; Ringo arrived with a poncho and toy guns. He said, "This town ain't big enough for both of us." Subsequently, Lancaster sent him two real guns and a holster.

Opposite: Brian Epstein encouraged the Beatles to end each show with a trademark perfect bow.

Above: Paul McCartney jokes with the rest of the band about how the Hollywood "meet and greet" is going to work.

Right: Caught in action, a furious George Harrison throws his drink at an unwanted photographer at the Whisky-A-Go-Go on Sunset Strip. Jayne Mansfield is sitting between George and John.

THE FIRST NORTH AMERICAN TOUR

The Beatles' first American tour was a resounding success and was on a much bigger scale than anything the Fab Four had witnessed before. No American act, not even Elvis, had created so much hysteria. Everybody who was there, in whatever capacity, has a vivid memory of what it was like.

"The shows were fun for me. They weren't fun if you were thinking of thirty thousand people who hadn't come to see you, but you didn't take it personally. I loved every minute of it. I did rousing songs like 'Shout,' and I was thrilled to be playing to that many people. I was in the middle of the show, and Brian Epstein moved me to closing the first half. I'd been able to control the crowd and get them listening to me. Obviously, having my child would be one of the big events of my life, but being on that tour would be up there in the Top Five. What a great honor it was."

JACKIE DESHANNON, SUPPORTING ACT (Left)

"Twenty thousand Beatlemaniacs pay so much—for so little. As a music critic I have had to subject my eardrums to more than a little of the cacophony which currently dominates the hit parade, but the stuff shouted by three Liverpudlian tonsorial horrors left me particularly unimpressed."

WILLIAM LITLER, *Vancouver Sun*

"The fans were pushing forward, and I could see that the makeshift stage was moving a little. Brian Epstein said, 'Red, you are the MC. I want you to get up there and tell the crowd to settle down or else the boys are going to leave.' I said, 'I can't do that,' and the chief of police said, 'You listen to Mr. Epstein—you're the MC, and you do that.' So I waited until the end of the song and then I walked across the stage, and John Lennon yelled at me, 'Get the fuck off our stage. Nobody interrupts the Beatles.' He's yelling at me, and I'm yelling back, just to be heard. I said, 'Brian has sent me up here.' John looked over, and Brian was giving him the OK sign. John then said, 'OK, carry on, mate.' My son said to me, 'Dad, it doesn't matter what you've accomplished. You will always be remembered in Vancouver as the man John Lennon told to fuck off the stage.'"

RED ROBINSON, MC AT EMPIRE STADIUM, VANCOUVER, AUGUST 22, 1964

"I worked with the Beatles when they first came to America. I had 18 dates with them and we were together for 21 days, including 3 days' vacation down in Key West, Florida. My manager, Bob Astor, got me on the bill, and Paul, Ringo, and myself and a guy with the Bill Black Combo got to be real good friends. We had a jam session down in Key West and I was showing them how to get that Louisiana sound."

CLARENCE "FROGMAN" HENRY (Right)

"We went to see them at the baseball stadium in Kansas City. Tom and I got our first jobs ever, so that we could afford the tickets. It was a Thursday night show, and I can see it now. The movie *A Hard Day's Night* had just come out. They said, 'Did you like the film?' and there was a huge roar. That was great. John was banging away on the stage and the heel came off his boot, but he didn't care, he kept on banging his foot. They were Elvis, and everybody else was turbocharged."

SCOTT McCARL, THE RASPBERRIES

"My grandfather was the manager of the Muehlebach Hotel [Kansas City]. It was a famous hotel, and it had been a host to some presidents. He told my parents that they could be in the lobby when the Beatles came, and it would be closed to everyone else. My grandfather checked in the Beatles, and he said that Paul was grumpy, but everyone is entitled to a bad day. My grandfather was besieged with neighbors who wanted anything they could get from the Beatles. He was asked for cigarette butts, but there weren't enough to go round. My grandfather and my grandmother smoked a few cigarettes and passed out some phony butts. They were approached by a marketing company to sell their bed sheets, which were then clipped into one-inch swatches and applied to a card which certified them as the official bed sheets of the Beatles."

ROBERT REYNOLDS, THE MAVERICKS

"No one had seen anything like them. They had long hair and strange accents and they were writing stuff that was really good. The one I really love is 'Tell Me Why' on *A Hard Day's Night*. The Beatles made everybody start writing because all we had been doing was covering songs. When we played in Hollywood clubs, we would always have to do the Number one record. The Beatles did covers too, of course, and they did them great."

GARY WALKER, THE WALKER BROTHERS

06 Red Rocks, Denver
Wednesday August 26, 1964

SHOWTIME 8 p.m.

ATTENDANCE 7,000 **CAPACITY** 9,450

Two radio stations tracked the band from Stapleton Field to the Brown Palace Hotel, encouraging a crowd of five thousand fans to gather. They were to play at the Red Rocks Amphitheater, a venue carved out of the rocks and opened

in 1906. This was Red Rocks' first rock concert as such, and alcohol had been banned following unruly audiences for Ray Charles and, believe it or not, Peter, Paul, and Mary.

The promoter Verne Byers had received this note from "Beatle Hater": "If you know what's good for you, cancel Denver engagement. I'll be in the audience and I'm going to throw a hand grenade instead of jelly babies." The FBI told them to continue with the concert, although the surroundings were such that a sniper on a hill could have shot any of them.

Above: Red Rocks Amphitheater was carved out of the rock, inspired by a natural amphitheater in Sicily.
Far left: Not everybody loved the Beatles and the FBI took this anonymous note (a photocopy from their files) very seriously.
Left: Ringo in full flow during the concert at Red Rocks Amphitheater, Denver, August 26, 1964.

For the press conference before the show, the promoter, KIMN, had wanted the Beatles to wear promotional cowboy vests, but McCartney refused. Joan Baez was scheduled to play at Red Rocks two nights later, and she flew in early to visit them. She had the Beatles singing along with "It Ain't Me Babe," and she gave Paul tips on finger-picking.

It was a good venue with a clear sound, but the Beatles found performing difficult. Because of the thin air at that altitude, oxygen canisters were on hand, although they weren't

needed. In contrast, the super-fit John Denver later was known to jog up and down the seventy rows before a concert.

One of the supporting acts, the Exciters, were booed for being black by one section of the crowd. They ran off stage, but then bravely returned to a standing ovation and went on to give the show of their lives.

07 Cincinnati Gardens
Thursday August 27, 1964

SHOWTIME 8 p.m.
ATTENDANCE 14,000 **CAPACITY** Oversold

The Beatles boarded their plane from Denver to Cincinnati at 10 a.m., and at the press conference, David Bracey of the Cincinnati Enquirer asked John what they would do when Beatlemania was over. John replied, "We'll count the money."

Cincinnati Gardens was a venue usually used for boxing bouts. It had poor ventilation, and to make matters worse, the audience was 20 percent over capacity. The heat was said to be 115 degrees F (46 degrees Celsius), and many fans fainted.

The Beatles were not staying and they boarded their plane for New York at 11 p.m.. It had been a taxing day, even by Beatles standards. And it wasn't over yet. A fan pulled off Ringo's St. Christopher medallion; after this was reported on WABC, it was returned later in the day.

Below: Police move in to disentangle a fan from around George Harrison during the Forest Hills concert.
Below right: The Forest Hills Music Festival was an impressive event, with major performers who would appeal to teenage kids, their middle-of-the-road parents, folkniks, and jazz aficionados.

08 Forest Hills, New York City
August 28 and 29, 1964

SHOWTIME 8 p.m.
ATTENDANCE 16,000 each night

Forest Hills wanted to ensure that no damage was done to the tennis courts, so they were covered with barricades. The old wooden stadium was shaped like a horseshoe, and a stage was set up for the Beatles behind the courts.

The Beatles were staying at the Delmonico on Park Avenue in Manhattan. The police advised them to travel by helicopter,

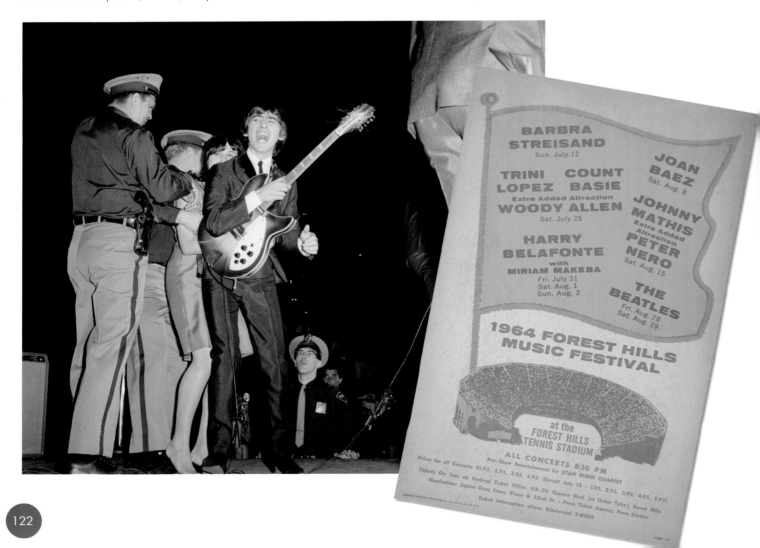

and the Beatles took off late from the Wall Street Heliport. As the Chinook became airborne, George said, "Beatles and children first." The shows were hosted by the WMCA Good Guys, who maintained the crowd's excitement with chants of "Give me a B," "Give me an E," and so on until they had spelled out the Beatles. The helicopter eventually landed behind the stage, and the Beatles started playing at 9:50 p.m.

One girl made a desperate sprint through the police cordon and made it onto the stage. She grabbed hold of George, who carried on playing with the girl's arms around his neck. Several more clambered onto the stage after her.

On Saturday, Al Aronowitz of the *Saturday Evening Post* brokered a meeting between Bob Dylan and the Beatles at the hotel. Dylan was amused by the Beatles; he recognized their melodic skill but was unsure of their talent. "Bob was sullen," said Aronowitz. "He thought they were bubblegum, but he came along anyway." Dylan asked for some cheap wine, but they only had champagne. Dylan suggested some pot. Although the Beatles were used to amphetamines from their time in Hamburg, they had smoked marijuana only once. This amused Dylan, who thought they had been singing "I get high" in "I Want to Hold Your Hand."

Still a little high, the Beatles did their second show at Forest Hills with improved security. The Beatles' Chinook helicopter arrived when the Righteous Brothers were on stage, so no one paid any attention to their performance. The duo had had enough. They performed the following night in Atlantic City and were then replaced by Clarence "Frogman" Henry. "Righteous indignation," quipped George Harrison.

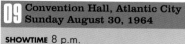

09 Convention Hall, Atlantic City
Sunday August 30, 1964

SHOWTIME 8 p.m.
ATTENDANCE 18,000 **CAPACITY** Sold out

A few days before the Beatles' Atlantic City concert, Lyndon Johnson had secured the Democratic presidential nomination for reelection in the Convention Hall, where the Beatles were

Above: The band had a few days off in Atlantic City, but didn't venture out of their hotel. Here, George Harrison is playing Monopoly with Jackie DeShannon, one of the tour's supporting acts.

due to play. The BBC news reporter Peter Woods had been in New Jersey for the nomination and stayed on to vacation with his family. He hadn't anticipated the Beatles' also staying at his hotel, the Lafayette Motor Inn. He broadcast a short interview with them in which he grouchily complained about the noise. "Well, you shouldn't stay in cheap hotels, should you?" John Lennon shot back.

Paul joked about Ringo for president, but Brian Epstein was adamant that the Beatles should not get involved in American politics. He declined a photo opportunity of the Beatles laying a wreath, with President Johnson, on Kennedy's grave.

Fortunately for the Beatles, Peter Woods failed to notice the parade of hookers going in and out of their hotel suite, although the reporter Larry Kane found they were making no secret of it. They assumed that no one travelling with them would give the game away. The tour manager, Bob Bonis, heard a mother telling her young daughter to find her way to a Beatle's bedrooms and shout "Rape!"—hoping for a payoff. Bonis tightened up the security.

The Beatles had a two-day break before their next show, but they did not leave the hotel suite. During their time in the Lafayette, Paul wrote "What You're Doing." Elvis Presley sent a goodwill telegram. Paul spoke on the phone to Elvis, who told him he was learning the bass but blistering his fingers. Paul told him to keep working at it.

11 State Fair Coliseum, Indianapolis
Thursday September 3, 1964

SHOWTIME 4 p.m. and 8 p.m.

ATTENDANCE 12,413 and 16,924

CAPACITY Both shows sold out

In Indianapolis, the Beatles stayed at the recently built Speedway Motor Inn, carefully guarded by state troopers. They were given a tour of the Indianapolis Motor Speedway and saw their first state fair, with its agricultural produce and farm animals.

The demand for tickets had been great, but the Coliseum was already booked for another event later that day, so a second concert was arranged around the grandstand, elsewhere on the State Fairgrounds. The Beatles received $85,000 for their day's work. John Lennon had a sore throat, so as a precaution all four were given antibiotics.

10 Convention Hall, Philadelphia
Wednesday September 2, 1964

SHOWTIME 8 p.m.

ATTENDANCE 13,000 **CAPACITY** Sold out

There was an elaborate plan to transport the Beatles the sixty miles from Atlantic City to Philadelphia without them being followed or mobbed on arrival. They left the Lafayette Motor Inn in a fish truck and switched to a bus just outside Atlantic City. Then they were taken to an underground garage next to the Philadelphia Convention Hall, which had been cleared for the day.

They gave their standard show, finding their best moments with the ballads. They announced "If I Fell" as "If I Fell Over." The Beatles received an ecstatic reception, and the audience stood on their chairs for most of the performance.

The famous psychic Jeane Dixon, who had predicted Kennedy's assassination, said that the Beatles' plane would crash. George Harrison called her up and said he found her "reassuring."

Left: A state fair would have been alien to the Beatles, although they might have seen the 1962 film starring Pat Boone and Bobby Darin. The closest event they would have known was the annual Liverpool Show at Wavertree Playground.

12 Milwaukee Arena
Friday September 4, 1964

SHOWTIME 7:30 p.m.

ATTENDANCE 11,500 **CAPACITY** Sold out

For the Beatles' flight into Milwaukee, the police had switched them from their original scheduled airport. The fans did not learn of the switch, so you might assume that the Beatles were relieved. Quite the reverse: they found it unfair, as they couldn't even wave to the fans. John Lennon missed the press conference because of his sore throat.

Considering their health, the concert went well, but the police kept the fans at a distance from the hotel. Their response was to yell loudly, so few local residents had a good night's sleep.

Top: The Beatles playing with a miniature race track. In this photograph, John is most interested—in keeping with his model railway back home in Kenwood.
Above: Unlike today, the tour program would be personalized for each of the venues.

125

13 International Amphitheater,
Chicago, September 5, 1964

SHOWTIME 8:30 p.m.
ATTENDANCE 13,000 CAPACITY Sold out

For their Chicago arrival, once again the airport was switched at short notice, but this time fans were alerted that the plane was coming into Midway. One hundred fifty journalists attended the press conference, which began with William Ludwig, Jr., giving Ringo a gold-plated drum, which he still possesses. Paul commented that he was hoping to meet some gangsters in Chicago. One girl, wearing a set of handcuffs, tried to get herself close to Paul so that she could lock the companion cuff around his wrist—nice try.

After two and a half weeks of touring, the Beatles looked rough and unwell. They were relieved that the plans for a civic reception during the afternoon were cancelled because of a shortage of policemen.

During the concert at the International Amphitheater, a raw steak was thrown at Paul. He ducked, and George kicked the steak out of the way. It wasn't the only odd missile: in addition to the inevitable jelly beans, a stuffed animal, a rubber ball, and a skipping rope found their way onto the stage. The atmosphere was hot and sticky, but the Beatles gave a very good show—perhaps, in part, because the ushers had been chosen based on their lack of interest in the Beatles.

14 Olympia Stadium, Detroit
Sunday September 6, 1964

SHOWTIME 2 p.m. and 6 p.m.
ATTENDANCE 15,000 each show, Sold out

In Detroit, an anti-Beatles brigade had mounted the slogan "Help stamp out Beatles," which Paul McCartney modified to "Help stamp out Detroit." This made him *persona non grata* in parts of Detroit, but the press conference took pains

Above: The Ludwig Drum Company gave Ringo this gold-plated snare drum in Chicago in appreciation of his loyalty to the brand.

to make it clear that the Beatles loved the city, and Tamla-Motown records in particular.

For the Detroit date, the Beatles played an ice hockey rink, the Olympia Stadium, which had a special surface laid for the concert. Two girls held up a banner: "We Are from Tuebrook" (a district in Liverpool). The police at the concert were authoritarian: they arrested forty jelly-bean throwers.

15 Maple Leaf Gardens, Toronto
Monday September 7, 1964

SHOWTIME 4 p.m. and 10 p.m.
ATTENDANCE 17,766 each show, Sold out

The scenes of chaos at Malton Airport in Toronto topped those in America. Ten thousand Canadian fans gathered for the Beatles and waited several hours. They were held back by a metal fence, which the security force and mounted police had problems in keeping upright. The Beatles had to make a quick exit—and all this was two hours after midnight. The fans stormed an armored car carrying the band to the King Edward Hotel, where both John and Paul were mobbed and

Paul's shirt was torn. A fourteen-year-old was found hiding in a linen cupboard in the hotel. The mayor of Toronto, Philip Givens, came to welcome the Beatles but was turned away by a blonde, leading to this memorable *Daily Star* headline: "Beatles Blonde Snubs Mayor."

The concerts were very well received, and in between the shows there was a brief press conference, at which John remarked, "We came over here to do a tour and work. We didn't come here to sightsee or see buildings or the local beauty spots." Despite that, Paul McCartney was seen filming the local scenery later in the day. During the show break the Beatles also met Canadian Beatles fan club presidents, as well as Miss Canada—who later joined them at their hotel after they were returned in a police wagon.

The Beatles were still concerned about segregation at the forthcoming concert in Jacksonville. Paul said, "We've all talked about this, and we all agree that we would refuse to play. We all feel strongly about civil rights and segregation."

Below: The security at the King Edward Hotel in Toronto could not contend with the sheer number of fans trying to get close to the Beatles. John and Paul were both mobbed, and here we can see George Harrison about to be waylaid by an excited teenager as he walks through the hotel lobby.

continued on page 133

Left: The Beatles held a press conference on stage in between their two Toronto concerts.
Opposite: John in shades and cap, looking every inch the rock star on his hotel bed in Toronto.
Below: A line of police join hands to hold back the crowd as the Beatles leave Maple Leaf Gardens, Toronto, after their shows on September 7, 1964.

THE WACKY WORLD OF BEATLES NOVELTY RECORDS

Every record label in America would have liked the Beatles in their catalog, but most had to make do with artists covering their songs and the fast-buck world of Beatles novelties.

THE PROBLEM WAS THE PROFUSION OF BEATLES NOVELTIES, and the question: would even the most ardent Beatle fan want to collect novelty records? Several did make the *Billboard Hot 100*, but none got far. This is not to say the records aren't interesting—quite the reverse: they form a picture of the times, and some very considerable talents were jumping onto this bandwagon. Who knows what Ella Fitzgerald was thinking when she recorded her own song, "Ringo Beat," for the prestigious Verve label, urging her listeners to "Come on and get with it"?

There had been Beatles novelties in 1963—one of them, the witty "Beatle Crazy," was by the American bluegrass performer Bill Clifton. It set the bar high for Beatles tributes. The British musical comedy star Dora Bryan made the UK Top 20 with the feeble "All I Want for Christmas Is a Beatle," while the Vernons Girls, from Liverpool, became the Carefrees and made the *Billboard* charts with "We Love You Beatles."

As America geared up for Beatlemania in early 1964, the record labels were already devising their tributes. One of the first artists was Sonny Curtis, who played with the Crickets, the band that had inspired the Beatles' name. Curtis says, "Lou Adler was a record producer who got me a deal with Dimension Records.

The Beatles were about to hit America, and so he and I wrote 'A Beatle I Want to Be.' It was so early that the record company didn't realize how the Beatles spelled their name and put 'BEETLES' on the label." [However, most pressings seem to have had Beatles spelled correctly.] A few months later, Curtis was picking on Lennon and McCartney with *Beatle Hits— Flamenco Guitar Style*, a much better album than its clumsy title would suggest.

Sonny Curtis's single is about Beatles envy; others include Bobby Wilding's "I Want to Be a Beatle" (though he sounds more like Del Shannon), and Murray Kellum's "I Dreamed I Was a Beatle"; Kellum's "Long Tall Texan" had inspired the Beach Boys.

Quite fortuitously, the star of *Bonanza*, Lorne Greene, recorded a western saga, "Ringo," about the gunslinger Johnny Ringo. The record had nothing to do with Mr. Starr—but its very title took it to the top of the U.S. charts. A New York comedian, Dick Lord, seized the moment and rewrote the song as "Like Ringo." In the song, Dick waits for his girlfriend's fling to pass, but he isn't prepared for the twist in the message of the final verse:

*"She said a foolish thing had passed
And now I knew the truth at last,
Between her sighs, her sobs, her moans,
She said she loved the Rolling Stones,
Not Ringo."*

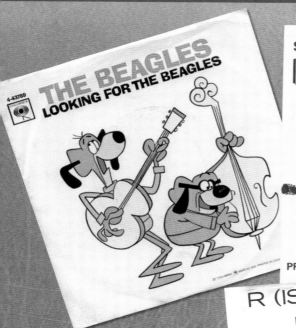

Left and below: UK singles rarely had picture sleeves in 1964, but most of the U.S. ones did, and the Beatles tributes were often attractively and amusingly packaged—indeed, the sleeves were quite often better than the records inside.

Although Phil Spector was producing classic tracks in 1964, he made the cheap single "Ringo I Love You" for "Bonnie Jo Mason," the first release from the singer who would become known worldwide as Cher. Four years later, Rainbo recorded "John, You Went Too Far This Time," and the critical fan whom Lennon was losing turned out to be the actress Sissy Spacek.

A song like "Ringo I Love You" illustrates the simplest way to write a tribute song. You take bits from million-selling compositions and string them together in one song, so although "Ringo I Love You" credits four songwriters on the label, it should have listed six (or two, depending on how you view it). Further examples are the Bootles with "I'll Let You Hold My Hand," the Beatlettes with "Yes, You Can Hold My Hand" and the Bagles with "I Want to Hold Your Hair." There is also an answer single to "I Saw Her Standing There": "Only Seventeen" by the Beatle-Ettes.

The Bagles' single is labeled *Meet The Bagles* and starts with an Ed Sullivan impersonation. The Rutles did it better, so "no, no, no," but the best record that incorporates snatches of Beatle songs is Nilsson's imaginative "You Can't Do That."

In March 1964 the Four Preps rewrote their hit, "Got a Girl" as the cynical "A Letter to the Beatles." According to the song,

the group was fleecing the public by charging for autographs and selling canine hair as "Beatle hair." The song incorporated snatches of "I Want to Hold Your Hand," and it is surprising that Capitol sanctioned such a critical track.

Capitol also released "My Boyfriend Got a Beatle Haircut" by Donna Lynn. Variations on this theme were legion, including "The Guy with the Long Liverpool Haircut" (The Outsiders), "The Beatles' Barber" (Scott Douglas), and a rare doowop tribute, "My Beatle Haircut" (Twiliters).

In 1963 the girl group the Angels topped the U.S. charts with "My Boyfriend's Back," but found it difficult to have hits once Beatlemania had struck. "Little Beatle Boy" was never going to do the trick. At the end of the first American tour, Gigi Parker and the Lonelies recorded "Beatles, Please Come Back," written by Chip Taylor, the composer of "Wild Thing."

There is a subgenre of Ringo Starr tributes, including several campaign records advocating Ringo for president, with one from Rolf Harris. When Ringo married Maureen Cox in 1965, Angie and the Chicklettes recorded "Treat Him Tender, Maureen." Neil Sheppard released "You Can't Go Far Without a Guitar (Unless You're Ringo Starr)."

Many of the tribute groups took their names from the Beatles, including the Beatlewigs, the American Beatles, and Benny and the Bedbugs, who released "Beatle Beat." And don't overlook the anti-Beatles records—although it's hard to tell whether they were aimed at Beatles fans or Beatles haters. They include the Exterminators with "The Beatle-Bomb," the Insects with "Let's Bug the Beatles," and an update to Buchanan and Goodman's "The Flying Saucer" with the Martians replaced by Beatles, made by Buchanan and (songwriter Howie) Greenfield. The final words are "America, this is the end."

Homer and Jethro turned "The Boll Weevil Song" into "Gonna Send 'Em Home," but they are to be commended for knowing that the Beatles actually got their U.S. start on *The Jack Paar Show*. On his *Songs for Swingin' Livers* album, the parodist Allan Sherman turned "Pop Goes the Weasel" into "Pop Hates the Beatles," and he performed it on TV with Dean Martin and Vic Damone. Martin couldn't have cared less, but Damone looks embarrassed as he sings:

"Ringo is the one with the drums,
The others all play with him,
It shows you what a boy can become
Without a sense of rhythm."

The majority of the Beatles tribute records were made in 1964. We would have to wait nearly a quarter of a century for the best of all: George Harrison with his very own tribute, "When We Was Fab."

Right: Long before karaoke, there were monthly songbooks of hit lyrics published in the U.S.. Here's a special issue devoted to the Beatles with a page of Beatles tributes—"My Boyfriend's Got a Beatle Hair Cut" (Donna Lynn), "We Love You Beatles" (The Carefrees), "The Beatles Hop" (Bret and Terry), "Beatle Fever" (Bret and Terry again), and "The Boy With The Beatle Hair" (The Swans). "We Love You Beatles" was originally written by Charles Strouse, the author of *Annie*, as "We Love You Conrad" for his 1960 satire about Elvis in the army, *Bye Bye Birdie*.

16 Forum, Montreal
Tuesday September 8, 1964

SHOWTIME 4 p.m. and 8 p.m.
ATTENDANCE 9,500 and 11,500 (Sold out)

17 Gator Bowl, Jacksonville
Friday September 11

SHOWTIME 8 p.m.
ATTENDANCE 23,000, but all
32,000 tickets sold

There had been strong anti-British feelings in Montreal for decades, and some French-Canadian separatists threatened to kill Ringo Starr because he was "an English Jew." As a result, Ringo (who, as it happens, isn't Jewish) was shadowed by a plain-clothes policeman throughout his time in Montreal; he even sat with him on stage.

Ringo placed his cymbals vertically in front of him for more protection (begging the question: if faced with a death threat, why put him on a high-rise stand at all?). He hunched low as he played, and later he said that the two shows in Montreal were the worst gigs of his life.

"I saw the Beatles in Montreal when I was ten years old," recalls comedy scriptwriter Gail Renard, "but not near enough to touch. I remember the screaming, and my mother forced my older brother to take me, as I couldn't go alone, and he didn't want to go, as he was a Beach Boys fan. It was magical, and John sang 'If I Fell' and fell to one knee as he was singing. They were clowning around, and it was wonderful. It was the local hockey arena, but it wasn't anything like the size of some of the hockey arenas today."

Their plane to Florida was diverted to land in Key West because of the 120-mph winds of Hurricane Dora that were battering the Jacksonville area. It was a 1,300-mile flight—Ringo started yet another pillow fight—and they arrived at 3:30 a.m., with very few fans aware of the change in plans.

For Jacksonville, the Beatles and their entourage stayed in a hotel in Key West, which was almost deserted, as it was out of season. They relaxed for a couple of days, swimming, sleeping, and jamming with other artists on the tour. The Beatles gave Bob Tucker of the Bill Black Combo $500 and asked him to buy some albums, which they listened to while there. A photograph of John Lennon swimming with the two girls from the Exciters was printed the day before the Gator Bowl concert—this was brave but dangerous, as there could have been repercussions from white supremacy groups like the Ku Klux Klan.

Jacksonville had been devastated by Hurricane Dora—buildings were damaged and palm trees uprooted—and even when the Beatles arrived, there were still fifty-mph winds,

Right: High winds were lashing the Florida coast in Jacksonville—those palm trees should be upright—even as the Beatles were traveling there from their concerts in Canada. The show was close to being cancelled.

133

Above: The effects of Hurricane Dora in Jacksonville: for the four boys from Liverpool, this must have been a frightening scene of devastation.

plenty of rain, and dark, brooding skies. President Johnson arrived on Air Force One to see the damage, and the Beatles' plane was not allowed to land until he had left.

A short press conference was held at the George Washington Hotel in Jacksonville. The Beatles weren't happy about this, as the segregated hotel had cancelled their reservations after finding that some of the party—specifically the Exciters and Clarence "Frogman" Henry—were black. After the press conference, it was over to the Gator Bowl, an outdoor venue—which created problems, given the weather, as the drum kit had to be nailed to the stage in the face of the furious wind.

Despite the Beatles' fears, there was no segregation at the concert, although most Beatles fans were white anyway. The venue had been sold out, but around one in four ticketholders decided the weather was too bad even to go see the Beatles.

There were unlicensed cameramen in front of the stage, and Derek Taylor came on to announce "The Beatles are a hundred feet away. They came thousands of miles to be here. The only thing preventing their appearance is the eight cameramen." The audience shouted "Out! Out! Out!" and the police forced the photographers to leave. When the Beatles finished their set, the audience was told that the Beatles were taking a break; they were actually on their way to the airport.

18 Boston Garden
Saturday September 12, 1964

SHOWTIME 8 p.m.

ATTENDANCE 13,909   **CAPACITY** Sold out

It was another long journey to Boston from Florida, but when they got there, the band's Madison Hotel was conveniently situated right next door to the ice hockey rink venue where they would be playing.

The tickets could have been sold several times over, and scalpers were selling them for a then-outrageous $50. Another entrepreneur seized the opportunity to catch the surplus demand by booking the Arena for a tribute band, the Minets, but only five hundred turned up.

This was an uncomfortable concert, as there was no air conditioning. For the first time on the tour, John played a twelve-string Rickenbacker guitar. Afterward, the Beatles were rushed to waiting cars for the trip to the airport, from which they flew south to Baltimore.

19 Civic Center, Baltimore
Sunday September 13, 1964

SHOWTIME 2:30 p.m. and 8 p.m.

ATTENDANCE 14,000 each show, Sold out

Two girls had themselves delivered to the Baltimore concert venue in a large box marked "Beatles fan mail." A security guard soon realized what the real contents were and the girls didn't manage to get themselves smuggled in, but it was certainly a very enterprising plan.

A guitar teacher from Baltimore, Tony Saks had a Rickenbacker 365 guitar and through a prior arrangement, he passed it to the Beatles for signature. This was professionally done by writing on gold leaf and lacquering over the handwriting. In the 1980s Saks took his guitar to Beatle conventions and eventually sold it in Japan.

20 Civic Arena, Pittsburgh
Monday September 14, 1964

SHOWTIME 8 p.m.

ATTENDANCE 12,603

The Pittsburgh concert came about through Pat DiCesare, a young record distributor, who borrowed $5,000 from his father as a deposit. The Beatles' fees were such that he had to charge $5.90 per ticket, but he knew the demand would be high. The concert took place in the world's first sporting arena with a retractable roof. The publicity said that the Beatles were going to raise the roof! The concert was a huge success, and the Beatles made $37,000.

21 Public Auditorium, Cleveland
Tuesday September 15, 1964

SHOWTIME 8 p.m.

ATTENDANCE 11,000

The Beatles arrived at the Sheraton-Cleveland Hotel the night before their Cleveland concert, and many fans tried to breach the intense security to reach the band. One hundred policemen attempted to keep fans from the Beatles as they performed, but still some managed to break through onto the stage. During "All My Loving" the police chief ordered the Beatles to stop playing and leave the stage so that the fans could calm down. Paul gave the crowd a thumbs-down sign.

Backstage, John Lennon said to a local radio DJ, "This has never happened to us before. These policemen are a bunch of amateurs." Brian Epstein said, more diplomatically, "The police were absolutely right. It was clear from the start that something was very wrong. The enthusiasm of the crowd was building up much too early."

Derek Taylor had the job of mediator again, and went on stage to speak to the fans. They paid attention to him, as he wasn't yelling at them as the police had, and settled down. After fifteen minutes, the concert continued without further

incidents, and then the Beatles flew to New Orleans. The authorities decided that the Beatles could not return to Cleveland and risk a repeat of the crowd behavior, so the city was not included in the 1965 tour. They did, however, return in 1966—and the outcome was even worse.

22 City Park Stadium, New Orleans
Wednesday September 16, 1964

SHOWTIME 9:30 p.m.

ATTENDANCE 12,000 **CAPACITY** Sold out

The Beatles landed in New Orleans early in the morning. A helicopter was to take them to Congress Inn; however, it was grounded with a mechanical failure, so limousines were dispatched—to the wrong airport. When they finally reached the Beatles, the police outriders became separated from the limousines, so the Beatles were surrounded by fans. As the police tried to control the situation, the limousine hit a police car. Eventually the Beatles got into the hotel, and Brian Epstein was horrified to find it was only a single-story building and in the midst of swampland.

There was a press conference, and the mayor of New Orleans, Vic Schiro, gave them the key to the city, but the Beatles were more impressed when they reached the football stadium and met the rhythm and blues legend Fats Domino.

The stage was far away from the audience, but during "Can't Buy Me Love" fans broke through the police line. John Lennon said, "We'd like to continue with our next number if you would stop playing football in the middle of the field." It took twenty minutes to restore order, and over two hundred fans collapsed through excitement and exhaustion. John Lennon ended the show by saying, "Thank you, folks—those of you who are still alive."

Musically, it was a poor show, as the microphones kept cutting out. And as the Beatles finished, rain began to pour; it was just as well the storm hadn't begun earlier, as the organizers had not arranged insurance cover for bad weather.

The Beatles peer through a clothes rail in Cleveland, September 15, 1964. The Beatles themselves are now key exhibits in The Rock And Roll Hall Of Fame in Cleveland.

23 Municipal Stadium, Kansas City
Thursday September 17, 1964

SHOWTIME 8 p.m.

ATTENDANCE 20,820

CAPACITY 41,000

24 Dallas Memorial Auditorium
Friday September 18, 1964

SHOWTIME 8 p.m. (started late at 8:15)

ATTENDANCE 10,500

Charles O. Finley was the owner of Kansas City Athletics, a very successful baseball team. An alpha male who got what he wanted, he had told Kansas City that he was booking the Beatles. He approached Brian Epstein soon after they arrived in the United States and offered $60,000 for the Beatles to play on their scheduled day off. Epstein said no. When Finley went to $100,000, Epstein still turned it down. Tearing up his check for 100 grand, Finley wrote another for $150,000, which the Beatles agreed to. It was easily the highest fee ever paid for a single performance at that time.

On the back of the tickets, Finley was pictured wearing a Beatle wig with the slogan, "Today's Beatles fans are tomorrow's baseball fans." The tickets did not sell as well as expected, although twenty thousand is still a huge crowd. The promoter wanted a longer set for his money, which he didn't get, but the Beatles did open with "Kansas City," which the crowd loved—and which the group had not yet recorded. In their excitement, the crowd surged onto the field. Finley lost $40,000 on the concert, but he felt like a winner just because he'd managed to book the Beatles, and although there was no profit, he gave $25,000 to a local children's hospital.

The Beatles stayed in the Muehlebach Hotel, where a girl who got trapped in the air conditioning had to be rescued by firemen. After the visit, their sheets was sold for $1,150. The hotel rooms were sealed until lawyers and witnesses were able to authenticate that these were indeed the Beatles' sheets—and whose bed each set of sheets had come from.

YEAH YEAH! YEAH!
TODAY'S BEATLE'S FANS
ARE
TOMORROW'S BASEBALL FANS

The Beatles were wary of going to Dallas. President Kennedy had been assassinated there less than a year earlier, and they had the impression that the city was gun crazy. Even the policemen guarding them were carrying rifles.

In fact, the police had a busy day the day the Beatles flew in, as both President Johnson and Republican presidential candidate Barry Goldwater were also in town—and even following part of Kennedy's route.

The Beatles received cowboy hats on their arrival at the airport, and they stayed at the Cabana Motor Hotel, which was co-owned by Doris Day. The Exciters were staying in the same hotel but, being black, they were not allowed through the front door. They had to take the service elevator to their rooms. Singer Pearl Bailey was also staying at the hotel, and she, too, was denied use of the front entrance.

The police had difficulty controlling the fans around the windows at the front of the hotel. Several girls fell through the windows, and three of them were seriously injured by the broken glass. The Beatles sent flowers and goodwill messages to the hospital the next day.

The Beatles gave their final press conference of the tour, which fans crashed by presenting identification letters for fabricated radio stations. A bomb threat delayed the start of the concert by fifteen minutes, but nothing was found, apart from fans hiding under the stage and in washrooms. A stage had been built three times higher than usual so that fans could not rush it and clamber on. There was an announcement, largely ignored, that if the fans threw anything the concert would be over.

Courtesy Mark Naboshek Collection

There had also been a threat of a bomb on the plane, but it left Dallas Love Field as scheduled at 11 p.m. A show at Colt Stadium in Houston on September 19 had been scrapped; instead, the Beatles spent a day on a ranch in Alton, Missouri, the guest of Reed Pigman, the owner of the charter airline American Flyers.

As they flew out of Dallas to Walnut Ridge, Arkansas, Paul sang "Happy Birthday" over the plane's loudspeaker to Brian Epstein, who was now thirty, and the boys gave him an antique telephone and water glasses as gifts. When they got to Arkansas, Pigman himself flew the Beatles to his ranch, where they landed in darkness on a field with just makeshift lights to guide the plane down.

The Beatles spent the day on a desert ranch in the Ozark Hills of South Missouri and went fishing and horseback riding. They rode for several hours, splashing through streams and across plains. Paul had another ride before they flew to New York, but he ended up bruised and saddlesore.

The New York plane was delayed because local dignitaries wanted autographs, but once on the flight from Dallas, the Beatles played and sang the tune that would become "Eight Days a Week"; they would record both it and "Kansas City" in October that year at Abbey Road, back in London.

Above left: The Beatles were wary of going to Dallas less than a year after Kennedy had been assassinated. How could they tell what was waiting for them? **Top and above:** The Beatles met with Fan Club reps in Dallas, and signed autographs (above) on their hotel notepaper.

25 Paramount Theater, New York
Sunday September 20, 1964

SHOWTIME 8:30 p.m.

ATTENDANCE 3,682

The final concert of the tour, "*An Evening with the Beatles*" had originally been scheduled for the Metropolitan Opera House. Its replacement, the Paramount Theater, had staged renowned concerts by Frank Sinatra and Benny Goodman and many rock 'n' roll package shows in the 1950s.

The artists for this event gave their services for free, as it was a benefit concert for charities supporting the Retarded Infants Services and United Cerebral Palsy. The official tour lineup had ended with the Dallas concert, so the acts for this show were not the same, and included Steve Lawrence and Eydie Gormé, the Shangri-Las, and Jackie DeShannon. The event was arranged by the radio station WABC, whose Ringo lookalike contest was won by a woman!

The Beatles flew by helicopter to the Wall Street Heliport, then on to the Paramount by limousine. Although there were only 3,700 patrons at the show, there were another 4,000 fans outside. And though the charity ticket prices began at a modest $5, there were 224 selling at $100. Many of the socialites in the exclusive seats did not approve of screaming teenagers, both inside and out. In view of the ear-piercing noise, the other acts were asked to shorten their sets, and the Beatles went on stage at 10 p.m. instead of 10:45.

The Beatles met Ed Sullivan backstage, and after the show they went to the Riviera Idlewild Hotel at Kennedy Airport. There was a farewell party with Bob Dylan, and a highly persistent Gloria Steinem got an interview with John Lennon for *Cosmopolitan*. Derek Taylor had an argument with

Brian Epstein over riding in his limousine and was sacked. Dedicated PR man Taylor had had enough of Epstein's tantrums, and despite his later apology, Taylor said he was leaving at the end of the year.

The Beatles flew home on the morning of September 21. Thousands of fans were at Heathrow to welcome them home, but the customs officers wanted $200 duty for the albums they were bringing into the country.

The British rock 'n' roll producer Jack Good was then making *Shindig* for American TV, and on October 2 he filmed the Beatles in a studio in Fulham, London, where they sang "Kansas City," "I'm a Loser," and "Boys." John Lennon played a harmonica on a holder for "I'm a Loser," a clear indication of Bob Dylan's influence. Jack Good described them as natural successors to the Crazy Gang.

Opposite: The Beatles would have been pleased to play the legendary Paramount Theater in Times Square, as its name was associated with Alan Freed's rock'n'roll package shows. This was a charity event and the tickets were not cheap, but still some young fans got to see them.
Above: This informal shot of the band was taken at the Paramount Theater, at the end of their long American tour. The band and everyone on tour with them was exhausted, but triumphant.

Brian Epstein was ecstatic about the tour's success and quoted impressive statistics to anyone who would listen. George Harrison was less comfortable, saying, "I feel sure we won't do another tour of the States for as long as five weeks ever again. It's so exhausting and not really satisfying for us." It had been an exhausting schedule. "Each of us lost seven pounds in sweat," said their roadie, Mal Evans. But ultimately, Brian Epstein had seen his prediction come true— the Beatles were, indeed, bigger than Elvis.

5 THE SECOND AMERICAN TOUR

"The Beatles played baseball stadiums with Vox AC somethings and 4 by 10 columns, which you would find in small discos or youth clubs today. They were using them as a PA for 50,000 people who were screaming as loud as they could. No one could hear them at all."

BRUCE DICKINSON, IRON MAIDEN

Left: A fantastic aerial view of the Beatles performing at Shea Stadium, Queens, on August 15, 1965. It is up there with Woodstock and Live Aid as the most historic and famous rock concerts of all time.

IN JANUARY 1965, BRIAN EPSTEIN RETURNED TO AMERICA TO DETERMINE THE DATES FOR THE NEXT TOUR. Presenting the group to an audience of twenty thousand in 1964 had intrigued him, so large stadiums became the norm. The strategy was hit and run—get the Beatles to the stadium by armored car, put them on stage, and once they were done, arrange their escape as quickly as possible. Epstein lined up $5.5 million in insurance for the safety of the Beatles with Lloyd's, recognizing that there was a risk that they might be torn apart by loving fans.

On the first tour, hardly anyone could hear the Beatles; on the second, hardly anyone would see them, as these were the days before big screens at concerts. Today's audiences would be furious if the main attraction couldn't be heard, couldn't be seen, and played for only half an hour. Concert technology had not changed much in the intervening year, but by the time the Beatles came back to New York on August 13, 1965, there had been other, significant changes. In June 1965 the Beatles had been officially recognized by the establishment, with MBEs bestowed by the Queen for their contribution to

British exports. In the United States, Bob Dylan, the Byrds, and others had created folk rock, and Dylan was now a major star. And the Vietnam war was escalating, with many teenage boys expecting their draft papers.

THE BEATLES ARE BACK

When the Beatles arrived at Kennedy International Airport, they were kept two miles from their fans. For security purposes this was ideal, but it made for poor publicity.

Opposite page: Police hold back the crowds as Buckingham Palace awaits the arrival of the Beatles to collect their MBEs.

Below: The Beatles display their MBEs. John Lennon looks happy enough for the photographers, but he was inwardly regretting accepting an award from the establishment. He gave it to Aunt Mimi and later claimed it back to return it to the Palace in 1969.

They were taken to the Warwick Hotel, where they took over the entire thirty-third floor. George Harrison called Mick Jagger to give him their private number at the hotel; he meant it as a private invitation, but later they learned his phone had been tapped, so now everybody knew the number.

The next day the Beatles filmed an appearance for *The Ed Sullivan Show.* "I Feel Fine," "I'm Down" (with John on organ), and "Act Naturally" were all in the first set, and "Ticket to Ride," "Yesterday" (solely Paul, with strings), and "Help!" were in the second. Lennon was on pills, but he pulled it together for the performance, although he stumbled on the lyrics of "Help!" John did, however, comment on Paul's solo of "Yesterday": "Boy, was he shitting himself." The recording was not broadcast until September 12, when it opened Sullivan's new season.

All of these songs except "Yesterday" were included in their stage set, and they added "A Hard Day's Night," "Can't Buy Me Love," "She's a Woman," "Dizzy Miss Lizzy," "Baby's in Black," and "Everybody's Trying to Be My Baby" (written by Carl Perkins as a joke, but it had relevance to Beatlemania). Ringo also sang "I Wanna Be Your Man." Often the Beatles would open with "Twist and Shout," but considering that this was only a two-and-a-half minute song, viewers may have wondered why they performed a truncated version.

The supporting acts for this tour were the Motown singer Brenda Holloway, Cannibal and the Headhunters (a Chicano band from East LA), the King Curtis Band with the Discotheque Dancers, and a British instrumental unit managed by Brian Epstein—Sounds Incorporated.

Right: A special edition of America's *16* magazine to celebrate the release of the Beatles' second film, *Help!* Everybody wanted to get in on the act, and here, even Superman is joking about the Beatles.

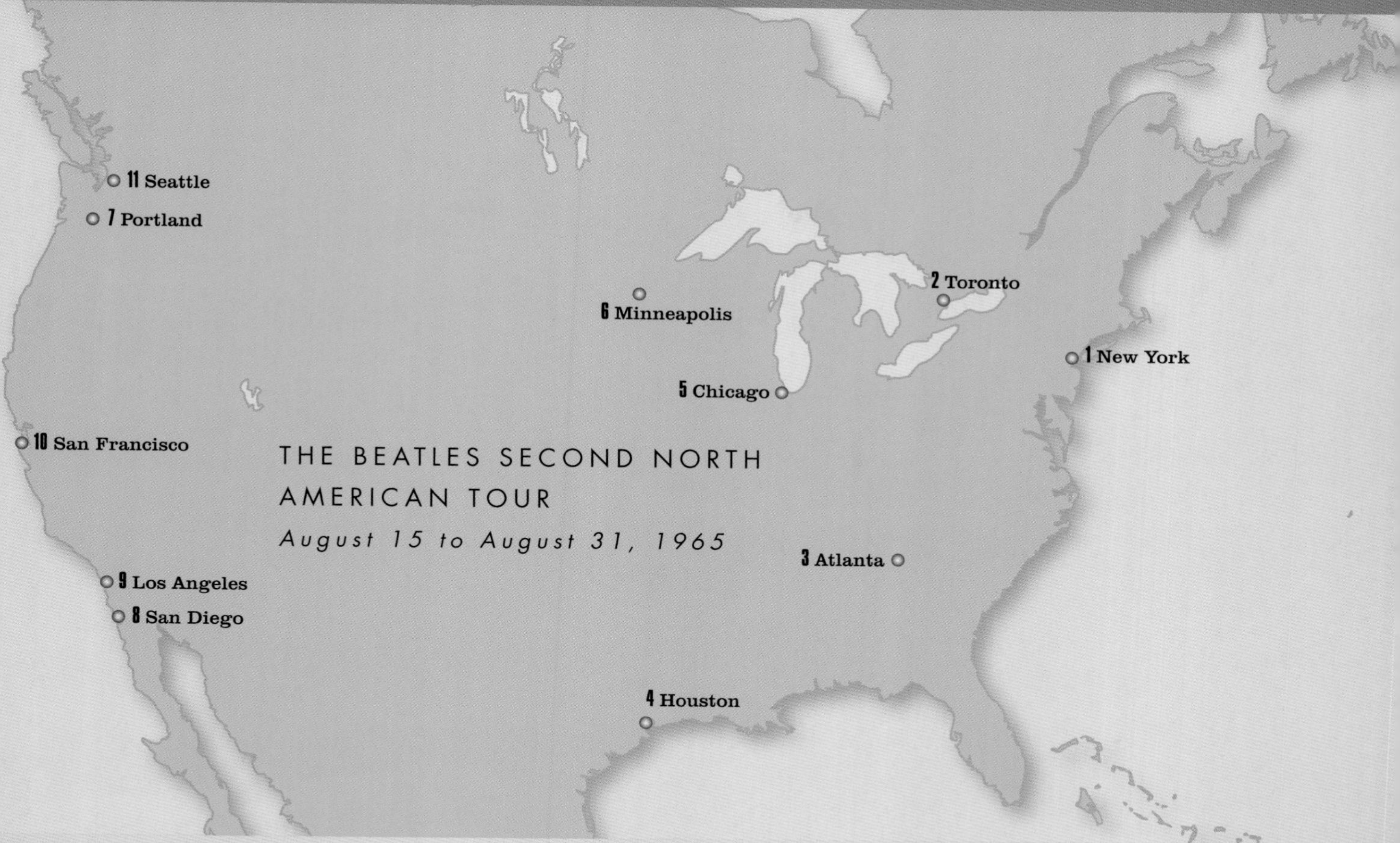

11 Seattle

7 Portland

2 Toronto

6 Minneapolis

1 New York

5 Chicago

10 San Francisco

THE BEATLES SECOND NORTH
AMERICAN TOUR
August 15 to August 31, 1965

3 Atlanta

9 Los Angeles

8 San Diego

4 Houston

01 Shea Stadium, New York City
Sunday August 15, 1965

SHOWTIME 8 p.m.

ATTENDANCE 55,600 CAPACITY Sold out

02 Maple Leaf Gardens, Toronto
Tuesday August 17, 1965

SHOWTIME 4 p.m. and 8:30 p.m.

ATTENDANCE 17,766 each show

03 Atlanta Stadium
Wednesday August 18, 1965

SHOWTIME 8:15 p.m.

ATTENDANCE 34,000 CAPACITY 51,500

04 Sam Houston Coliseum, Houston
Thursday August 19, 1965

SHOWTIME 3:30 p.m. and 8 p.m.

ATTENDANCE 12,000 each show

05 Comiskey Park, Chicago
Friday August 20, 1965

SHOWTIME 3 p.m. and 8 p.m.

ATTENDANCE 25,000 and 37,000

06 Metropolitan Stadium,
Minneapolis, August 21, 1965

SHOWTIME 7:30 p.m.

ATTENDANCE 28,500 CAPACITY 40,000

07 Memorial Coliseum, Portland
Sunday August 22, 1965

SHOWTIME 3:30 p.m. and 8 p.m.

ATTENDANCE 20,000 each show

08 Balboa Stadium, San Diego
Saturday August 28, 1965

SHOWTIME 8 p.m.

ATTENDANCE 17,013 CAPACITY 27,041

09 Hollywood Bowl, Los Angeles
August 29 and 30, 1965

SHOWTIME 8 p.m. each day

ATTENDANCE 17,256 each day

10 Cow Palace, San Francisco
Tuesday August 31, 1965

SHOWTIME 2 p.m. and 8 p.m.

ATTENDANCE 11,700 and 17,000

01 Shea Stadium, New York City
Sunday August 15, 1965

SHOWTIME 8 p.m.
ATTENDANCE 55,600 **CAPACITY** Sold out

KEY CONCERT: SHEA STADIUM

For their second tour, Brian Epstein was presenting the Beatles in the biggest venues possible, and the daddy of them all was Shea Stadium.

FIRST, SID BERNSTEIN HAD TO CONVINCE THE METS, the baseball team that played at Shea Stadium, as this would be the first music event ever held there and the largest audience to date anywhere for a pop concert.

There was a logistical problem in getting the band from their hotel to the stadium, as the streets would be full of fans. The obvious solution was a helicopter, but the Shea management would not allow a helicopter to land on the field. Alf Bicknell, the Beatles' driver, recalled, "We went from the hotel to the waterfront, where they had a heliport— an airport for helicopters, who would have believed it? We climbed in and flew over New York City, which was incredible. We landed on top of the World's Fair Building and took the lift to the ground. Then a Wells Fargo armored truck took us into the stadium." As they flew over the ground, the Beatles were amazed by the sight of thousands of fans taking photographs with flashbulbs. The truck took them into an area underneath the stadium, from where they could enter their dressing room.

I'M A
BEATLE FAN
In Case of EMERGENCY
CALL **PAUL**
OR **RINGO**

The Beatles made their way from their dressing room to the first base dugout; then, after being announced by Ed Sullivan, they ran to the stage, over second base. They were wearing smart beige uniforms, emulating those that Paul had admired on the military in Nassau, to which they had added Wells Fargo badges given to them by the driver of their armored car. The audience included a young Meryl Streep, the BBC presenter Brian Matthew, and Mick and Keith from the Rolling Stones, who had cruised to New York on a yacht with their manager, Andrew Loog Oldham. Also in the audience were two future Beatle wives—Linda Eastman (Paul) and Barbara Bach (Ringo).

It was a hot, sticky night, and soon the Beatles were sweating heavily in their buttoned-up uniforms. Over one hundred fans fainted and were treated by paramedics. Few of the audience remained in their seats; but those who broke out and rushed toward the stage were quickly tackled by guards. Murray the K was the MC for the concert, but Sid Bernstein introduced Ed Sullivan, who announced the Beatles.

The concert was simply a wall of noise. "You couldn't hear the music," says Sid Bernstein, "but you could hear the roar of the crowds in the Bronx—Shea Stadium is in Queens." Ed Sullivan's company was making a film of the concert for television, using several cameras. The visuals were fine, but overdubs of the singing—which were kept secret, as that was breaking union rules in the U.S.—had to be done later, in a studio. The dubbing didn't always work as it should—if you can find it online, marvel at how Ringo manages to sing parts of "Act Naturally" with his mouth shut! The film was not screened until May 1966 in the United Kingdom and, later still, January 10, 1967 in the U.S..

John Lennon made a great show of playing his Vox organ during the concert, including unorthodox notes played with his elbow. All four members of the band exaggerated their expressions and gestures to play up to the large audience in this vast arena.

Brian Epstein was crying tears of joy as they performed. And well he might: the concert grossed $304,000, and as the Beatles received 60 percent of the take, they exceeded what they had made at Kansas City, their previous record. Despite this, Bernstein actually lost money on the concert because of the excessive costs

Above and opposite: The pictures are evidence of the hysteria in the audience at Shea Stadium. Everything went right both here and on the rest of the tour, but even with the best planning and organization, there was plenty of potential for things to go wrong.

of security and his failure to budget for the helicopter that was needed to get the band there in the first place. Sid recalled, "Brian was very upset when he heard that and he wanted to give me a gift. I said, 'Brian, your gift was in giving me the boys.' Years later, John sat with me at a concert I produced for Jimmy Cliff and he said, 'Sid, I saw the top of the mountain with Shea.'" It had certainly been an extraordinary achievement.

The day after the concert had been left free. If it had rained on the scheduled night the concert would have been cancelled and reorganized for the following day. This left the band with a rare day of leisure. Back at the Warwick Hotel, the Beatles stayed "at home" in their rooms and met Bob Dylan, the Ronettes, Del Shannon, the Rolling Stones, the Exciters, and the Supremes. It was better for the Beatles to have a stream of visitors than to be left on their own, as they were prone to argue among themselves if they were left cooped up for too long.

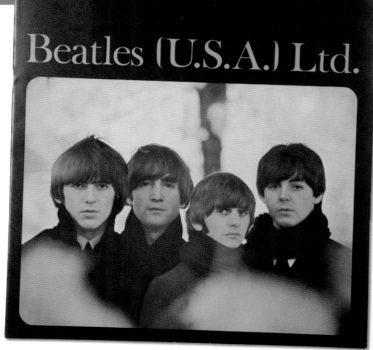

Beatles (U.S.A.) Ltd.

02 Maple Leaf Gardens, Toronto
Tuesday August 17, 1965

SHOWTIME 4 p.m. and 8:30 p.m.
ATTENDANCE 17,766 each show

In Toronto, the Beatles were on their usual form with quips and one-liners. From the press conference:

Reporter: "How did you propose to your wife?"
Ringo: "Same as anybody else. Are you married? If you're not married, find out."
Reporter: "I want to be married but I want to do it right."
Ringo: "You want to do it right?"
John: "Use both hands."

During the gap between shows, George Harrison complained that his and John Lennon's guitars were out of tune in the afternoon performance. He said, "There's such a tremendous noise that if you try and put it right, it ends up more out of tune than when you started. I've been thinking of getting Keith Richards to tune up for all of us. He always sounds in tune, and I have a hell of a lot of trouble."

03 Atlanta Stadium, Georgia
Wednesday August 18, 1965

SHOWTIME 8:15 p.m.
ATTENDANCE 34,000 **CAPACITY** 51,500

The Atlanta Stadium was another fifty-five-thousand-seat venue, but it was not sold out. The Braves were scheduled to move from Milwaukee to Atlanta and would play in this new stadium, but the transfer was delayed, so the first event to be held there was the Beatles' concert.

The South was still plagued with racial bigotry and segregation; in 1964 Lester Maddox had shut down his restaurant in Atlanta rather than serve black customers; he became the subject of Randy Newman's song "Rednecks." In Atlanta, John Lennon was photographed holding a magazine with the headline "The White Problem in the USA."

Above: The cover of the tour program for the 1965 tour.

Paul Drew, from local radio station WQXI-AM, was determined that the Beatles would have a good sound. When the Beatles heard how good it was for Cannibal and the Headhunters, they were impressed. Paul McCartney told the audience, "Ooh, it's loud. Isn't it great?"

The air conditioning and backstage facilities were not so good: the Beatles were given cots to relax on. Ringo leapt onto one and sucked his thumb. They liked the food, though, and signed the plates for the caterers (so if you see a dirty autographed plate offered on eBay as a genuine 1965 Beatles-play-Atlanta memento, it could be for real).

04 Sam Houston Coliseum, Houston
Thursday August 19, 1965

SHOWTIME 3:30 p.m. and 8 p.m.
ATTENDANCE 12,000 each show

The Beatles arrived in Houston at 2 a.m. The security, not helped by the dark, was terrible. Fans broke through the police lines toward the plane as it was still taxiing, running the risk of being cut to pieces by the revolving propellers.

BBC presenter Brian Matthew was on board: "We landed in Houston, and there were some very funny little airfields in America. Some were no more than dirt strips with a couple of buildings. Houston was like that. There was a gang of kids to meet the Beatles, and they not only surrounded the plane, they jumped onto it. They were on the wings, flicking cigarette butts about, and it was terribly dangerous. We weren't allowed off for some time." As it happens, contrary to Matthew, Houston's Hobby Airport was not one of the "dirt strips" he refers to, but a well-appointed modern airport.

The police determined that the Beatles would have to leave via the luggage exit, and they got them out after forty minutes of mayhem. Alf Bicknell was knocked off balance when someone threw a lighter at him. Lloyd's of London could have been paying out on that insurance policy.

The concert was MC'd by Russ "The Weird Beard" Knight who was shouting like a teacher trying to keep his class quiet. John Lennon's voice sounded rough on "Twist and Shout," and Paul and George could be seen laughing it off, which the Beatles often did when things went wrong.

continued on page 156

Below: The Beatles play to 12,000 fans in Houston —one of the smaller venues on this tour of vast arenas.

THE BUTCHERED COVER

An Australian photographer, Robert Whitaker, who was employed by Brian Epstein, was looking for new ways to capture the Beatles. By 1965, they were no longer interested in squeaky-clean publicity portraits and welcomed a challenge.

BOB WAS AN ADVENTUROUS PHOTOGRAPHER with a love of surrealism, and he wanted to pose the band wearing butchers' white jackets and holding dismembered dolls. Speaking in 2003, Whitaker recalled, "I had travelled with the Beatles, and I had watched the fans shouting and screaming at them, and I thought long and hard about a series of pictures showing that the Beatles were as normal as anybody in the room. When Moses came down from Mount Sinai carrying the Ten Commandments, he found people worshipping the golden calves—that is, the false images. All I wanted to do was show that the Beatles were made of flesh and blood.

I put in other pieces of Dadaism and surrealism, quoting Oppenheimer's *Lunch in Fur*, which is a teacup and saucer made

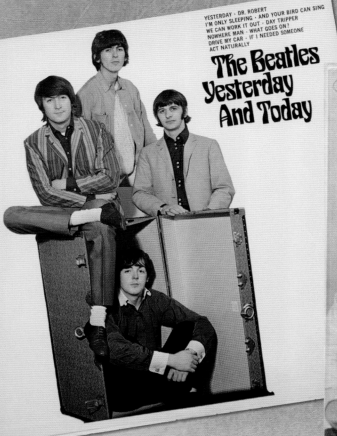

Below and left: The original and controversial butchers sleeve for the *Yesterday and Today* album, and its less alarming replacement.

from fur. I had George banging nails into John's head as though John were a wooden statue. The front cover would be a photograph of a girl with her back to the camera, and sausages were meant to be coming out of her nether regions like an umbilical cord. When I finished the shoot and the pictures were processed, they were sent to America, as Capitol was screaming out for an LP cover."

The "butcher" image that was put on the front of the compilation album *Yesterday and Today*, released in June 1966, was actually meant to be on the back of a gatefold. But seemingly without consideration of the likely response, Capitol decided to use it for the front. Many saw the original cover as a comment on American forces in Vietnam, but this was not Whitaker's intention. Nor was it a comment on what the Beatles thought of Capitol's releases, however tempting that theory may be.

The choice of image caused an outcry and Capitol quickly replaced the shocking cover with a new and uncontroversial

photograph (see opposite). But for some runs of the albums, the replacement cover was simply pasted over the butcher photo, and word got out that purchasers of those copies could, with skilful application, peel off the top photo to reveal the original. Ironically, the most valuable records today are the ones with the stuck-on replacement still intact, though it's hard to believe many fans could resist the urge to peel it away.

In 1965 the back cover of *The Rolling Stones, Now!* had created controversy, as in the liner notes, Andrew Loog Oldham had suggested that fans rob beggars for cash to buy the album. *Yesterday and Today* was the first controversial album front cover and the first of many such controversies to follow, including the debate over *Sgt. Pepper* within EMI as to whether Jesus, Gandhi, and Adolf Hitler could appear on the sleeve (they couldn't), the Rolling Stones' *Beggars Banquet*, and Blind Faith's one and only LP. And many stores refused to stock John and Yoko's *Two Virgins* with their nude photograph on the cover.

Above and left: Directly employed by Brian Epstein, the Australian photographer Robert Whitaker took a series of surreal images of the Beatles during the photo shoot that produced the infamous "butcher" image.

THEY'VE MET THE QUEEN, NOW MEET THE KING

It sounds like a momentous occasion: two heavyweights of popular music coming together for a rare meeting, but when the Beatles were invited to visit Elvis it was a surprisingly low-key affair.

WHEN IT CAME TO VISITING ELVIS PRESLEY, showbiz protocol dictated who would visit whom. The lesser star usually visited the bigger star, but who was the bigger: Elvis or the Beatles? This was a private meeting, though, so protocol shouldn't have mattered, and Chris Hutchins of the *New Musical Express* went to Paramount Studios to make the necessary arrangements with Colonel Parker. On August 27, the Beatles would go to see Elvis in Perugia Way, Beverly Hills, in a Frank Lloyd Wright house he had hired from the Shah of Iran while making a film.

The Beatles went with Brian Epstein, Mal Evans, Neil Aspinall, Tony Barrow, and Alf Bicknell, and when they saw Elvis they were impressed, not just because he was Elvis but because he had a remote control for his TV. They hadn't seen one before. Colonel Parker's opening words were "A chair for Mr. Epstein." He was amazed that Epstein managed several other acts:

Parker's time was devoted solely to Elvis. The conversation was fairly inconsequential. Elvis said of his films, "I play a country boy with a guitar who meets a few girls along the way, and I sing a few songs." He said that when they deviated from the formula, as with *Wild in the Country*, the films didn't do as well. Elvis played "Mohair Sam" by Charlie Rich on his jukebox. He called for instruments to be brought out—Ringo had bongos—and they jammed for a little while, starting, oddly, with Cilla Black's "You're My World."

But not much happened. George shared a joint with Larry Geller, who had a curious dual role as Elvis's hairdresser and spiritual advisor. Ringo and Mal Evans played pool with Jerry Schilling and Billy Smith, part of Elvis's "Memphis Mafia". Colonel Parker and Brian Epstein played roulette. Tony Barrow was disappointed, later describing Elvis as "a boring old fart." They recalled seeing his girlfriend, Priscilla, walking around in a long dress and tiara like a Barbie doll.

The Beatles were each given a pack of Elvis records as they left, and John shouted, "Long live the King!" Once inside the limousine, John confided to George that Presley was stoned, and George replied, "Aren't we all?"

Elvis was invited to see them the next day, but just a few of his Memphis Mafia went. They were also invited to the Hollywood Bowl concert, but that would have been a step too far—their loyalty was to Elvis. Elvis later denounced the Beatles for their subversive views and, somewhat hypocritically, their drug taking. But he gave them a mention in "Never Been to Spain" (1972), and he sang "Yesterday," "Hey Jude," and "Get Back" (in a medley with "Little Sister") on his return to splendor in Las Vegas.

Opposite page: The only known photograph of Elvis meeting the Beatles is this grainy and indistinct shot of them leaving: no press photographers were invited to record the event.

Above and top: Mutual appreciation society? Elvis was never too sure about the Beatles and he certainly regarded them as the biggest threat to his supremacy. They had different approaches to stardom: he was on a pedestal, the unobtainable star, while they were the boys next door. He was in artistic limbo in 1965 and envied the Beatles' success.

05 Comiskey Park, Chicago
Friday August 20, 1965

SHOWTIME 3 p.m. and 8 p.m.
ATTENDANCE 25,000 and 37,000

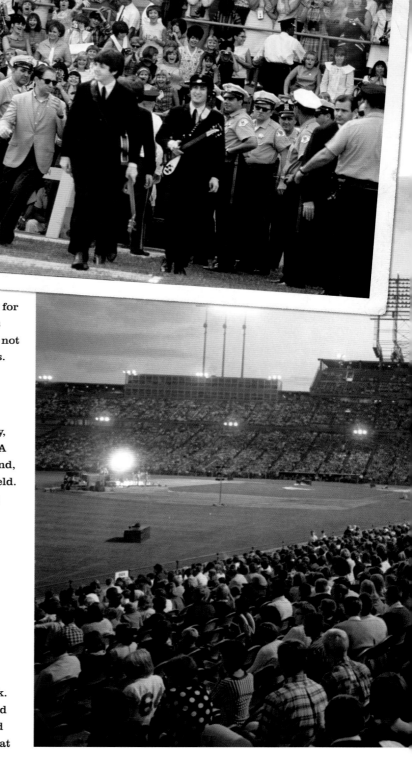

The Beatles arrived in Chicago on an early morning flight from Houston. Even though it was 3 a.m., there were hundreds of fans at the O'Hare Sahara Inn, because the management had foolishly announced the Beatles were staying there. Two radio stations, WLS and WCFL, were competing with each other for the latest information. At the press conference, the Beatles lamented the way that Capitol was releasing their albums, not following the UK order of play. John said, "We plan albums. We plan which number should follow each one."

It was a wild audience, as the attendants were instructed only to tell people to sit down, not to attempt to curtail their building hysteria. John played "I'm Down" in a frenzy, putting one foot up on the keyboard like Jerry Lee Lewis. A priest saw them in the interval and told them dirty jokes and, during the second show, a nude woman raced across the field. After the concert, some fans took bits of turf for souvenirs; others actually took their seats.

06 Metropolitan Stadium, Minneapolis
Saturday August 21, 1965

SHOWTIME 7:30 p.m.
ATTENDANCE 28,500 **CAPACITY** 40,000

In 1964, a department store in Minneapolis had contacted NEMS and asked them for a group for their Liverpool week. NEMS sent the Remo Four, and they played to shoppers and were featured on local radio. Colin Manley, the group's lead guitarist, told Ron Butwin, the owner of *B Sharp Music*, that

Left: Just another day in the life … The Beatles entertained a total of 62,000 fans in Chicago on August 20, 1965.
Below: It's still an enormous crowd, but you can see the empty seats in the Minneapolis Metropolitan Stadium.

George Harrison would have liked the Rickenbacker twelve-string. The owner gave one to George during the Minnesota press conference, which was broadcast live. Harrison was delighted, but didn't actually use the guitar until he was back in the United Kingdom. The Rickenbacker was featured on "If I Needed Someone," but George lost it after the Candlestick Park concert in 1966.

Backstage at the stadium, the Beatles experienced a sauna for the first time, but it was uncomfortable in Minneapolis because of a plague of mosquitoes. Radio station WDGY was copromoting the concert; when DJ Bill Diehl told the audience that the concert would end if the stage was rushed, he was booed. A rival radio station KDWB hired a helicopter to fly over the stadium, flashing the station's call letters while the Beatles were performing. John didn't sing "Twist and Shout," as he was hoarse, but he did add "Love me 'til I'm satisfied" to "Dizzy Miss Lizzy." After the concert, the Beatles left in a laundry truck for Minneapolis.

John wrote in one of his songs, "You can always get a simple thing like love anytime," but it wasn't always that easy, not even for a Beatle. Roadies Mal Evans and Neil Aspinall usually had the task of finding girls for the boys while they were away on tour, but they were not always successful. Paul was more fortunate, or maybe less, depending on how you look at it. The police knocked on his hotel door in the early morning in Minneapolis and accused him of having sex with an underage girl. His companion at the time was the fan club secretary from Cleveland, and she established that she was twenty-one. Paul was instead charged with making a "false hotel reservation." McCartney said he would never go back to the city, but he did return with Wings in 1976.

continued on page 162

THE BEATLES CARTOON

When an unknown artist pitched an idea for a Beatles cartoon to King Features, makers of Popeye, he was turned down, but a chance meeting as he waited for the elevator to take him out, changed the face of the band, if not the fortunes of the artist.

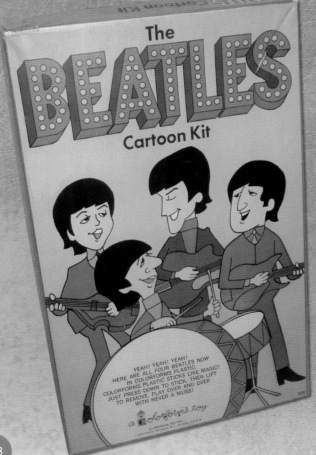

THE HEAD OF THE COMPANY, a Hungarian-American named Al Brodax, joined him in the hall, saw the drawings and thought his commissioning editor had made a mistake, but he didn't say so to the artist.

Instead, Brodax developed a plan of action and took it straight to Brian Epstein. The concept was to make a series of cartoons featuring the Beatles and their music. The stories would be based around their song titles, and the cartoon Beatles would be lip-synched to the records. Epstein gave him the animation rights, with the option for a full-length cartoon if they were successful. The series was directed by George Dunning, and much of it was created in Sydney and London rather than Hollywood.

The Beatles was sold to ABC-TV, who had their own requirements. They thought that replicating the Beatles' Liverpool accents might make the cartoon hard for children to understand, so they insisted on mid-Atlantic accents, instead. John and George's parts were voiced by Paul Frees, who also voiced the Jolly Green Giant, while the British actor Lance Percival, from the UK TV satire show *That Was The Week That Was*, voiced Paul and Ringo. Ringo had the most cause for complaint, as his character is depicted as essentially dopey, though lovable. In one episode, "*Money,*" his mother was said to have dropped him as a baby.

Above and left: The Beatles cartoon series was aimed at pre-teens, although older fans would naturally watch it as well. The images of the four cartoon Beatles were marketed in many forms, such as these candy bars (top) and a kit to play out your own Beatles storylines.

The Beatles were unhappy with the idea of the cartoon series, and the contract was signed with a stipulation that it would not be shown in the United Kingdom. It was the first time that a cartoon series had been made with animated versions of living people, and despite their reservations, the Beatles were photographed with their cartoon counterparts (overleaf).

The Beatles cartoon series began running on Saturday mornings in September 1965, and, with repeats, it carried on running until September 1969. There were thirty-nine half-hour episodes. They were trite and made too hurriedly, but children loved them. Playing to the Beatles' cuddly moptop image, the series enjoyed a 45-percent share of the audience.

That might have been the end of it, but Brodax knew that the Beatles were reluctant to make a third film for United Artists after *A Hard Day's Night* and *Help!*. He suggested making a

Above: John Lennon has a chance to view the cartoon images in London, December 1964. The Beatles themselves were barely involved with the planning or production of the cartoon series.
Overleaf: The Beatles posing on front of life-sized versions of their cartoon counterparts—and not looking too happy about it.

full-length cartoon instead. The Beatles agreed, expecting that it would be more of the same. But Brodax assembled a brilliant and innovative team and made *Yellow Submarine*. The rushes were so good that the Beatles knew they would be wrong to ignore it. They added a live coda to the film.

Yellow Submarine is a groundbreaking animated film including techniques that had not been seen before. Without the draw of the Beatles—and, indeed, of *The Beatles* cartoon series—the film would never have been made.

07 Memorial Coliseum, Portland
Sunday August 22, 1965

SHOWTIME 3:30 p.m. and 8 p.m.

ATTENDANCE 20,000 each show

The Beatles' flight from Minnesota to Portland arrived in the mid-afternoon. Just before they landed, one of the engines caught fire. John was pawing at the door in a panic, trying to get out. George said dryly, "This should stop them asking how much longer we are going to last."

At the press conference, Paul said they were not communists but Capitol-ists. Two more Capitol-ists, Carl Wilson and Mike Love of the Beach Boys, visited the Beatles in their dressing-room at the concert. And Allen Ginsberg was in the audience and wrote a poem about the show, "Portland Coliseum."

The Beatles flew on to Los Angeles just before midnight on August 22, 1965—on a replacement plane after the drama of the fire the previous flight. On arrival, they took a few days off in Benedict Canyon, North Hollywood, staying in a large house owned by Zsa Zsa Gabor. They were visited by Eleanor Bron, who'd had a role in *Help!*, and Joan Baez, a frequent visitor both backstage and wherever the band was staying. They befriended David Crosby of the Byrds, a good connection for drugs and, as it happened, for Indian music.

While the Beatles were swimming in Gabor's pool, they saw a helicopter circling until the pilot found them. It had been hired by "Beatle people" (the Beatles' term for fans). The pilot couldn't land, as the house was on a steep hillside, but the Beatles would have welcomed them: they admired ingenuity.

George told a visiting Peter Fonda that he feared he was dying. Fonda said later, "I told him there was nothing to be afraid of and all that he needed to do was relax. I said that I knew what it was like to be dead because when I was ten years old I'd accidentally shot myself in the stomach, and my heart stopped beating. John heard me saying, 'I know what it's like to be dead.'" This led to the song, "She Said She Said." But after two days they had tired of Fonda's stoned ramblings and barred him from the house.

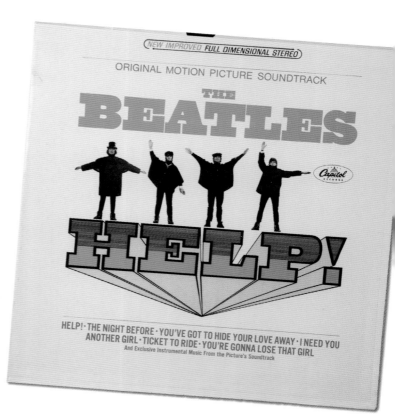

The Beatles watched *Cat Ballou*, starring Peter's sister, Jane, in a drive-in print with dubbed laughter and *What's New Pussycat?* John was playing Gene Vincent's "Be Bop A Lula" over and over and Paul and George attended a Byrds recording session for "The Times They Are A-Changin'."

08 Balboa Stadium, San Diego
Saturday August 28, 1965

SHOWTIME 8 p.m.

ATTENDANCE 17,013 **CAPACITY** 27,041

The Beatles travelled by bus from LA to San Diego. The concert there, which had replaced a date in Mexico City, had 10,000 unsold seats. At the press conference, George said that before a concert, "We usually scrub our feet, comb our hair, and have a cup of tea." On the return journey, the bus broke down and they went to a nearby mortuary, where they got into limousines to complete the trip.

09 Hollywood Bowl, Los Angeles
August 29 and 30, 1965

SHOWTIME 8 p.m. each day

ATTENDANCE 17,256 each day

10 Cow Palace, San Francisco
Tuesday August 31, 1965

SHOWTIME 2 p.m. and 8 p.m.

ATTENDANCE 11,700 and 17,000

If San Diego was a little lacking in sparkle, two excellent concerts followed, in the picturesque setting of the Hollywood Hills. While they were there, the Beatles were presented with a gold disc for $1 million in sales of the *Help!* album, and John Lennon commented, "Give us the money." Some fans jumped into the pool of water in front of the stage, and there was a poolside party for the press after the second show. The Beatles earned $90,000 for the two nights, and they were recorded by Capitol for a potential live LP.

Opposite: The Beatles second film, *Help!*, opened in America in August 1965. The UK album featured seven songs from the film with some additional tracks, while the U.S. version shown here had the film songs with incidental music from George Martin and his orchestra.
Below: In 1964, a nine-inch figure of each Beatle was issued by Revell Toys, a company which prided itself on making accurate scale models. A pristine set today is likely to fetch $4,000 at auction.

There is footage of John singing the old Jesse Fuller song "San Francisco Bay Blues" to himself as the Beatles exit the plane upon their arrival at the city airport.

Despite the problems at the Cow Palace concert the previous year, there were still not enough police officers. Fans climbed onto the stage, and there could have been a riot. Alf Bicknell and Joan Baez pitched in to ferry kids to safety, and thirty fans were hurt. The Beatles had to leave the stage for a few minutes. Backstage in between shows, George played "Greensleeves" while Johnny Cash and Joan Baez sang.

There was a small party at the Cabana Motor Hotel in Palo Alto, and Brian Epstein told John Lennon not to smoke pot in public. The Beatles thought that this would be their final U.S. concert, but Brian Epstein had other ideas.

6 THE THIRD AMERICAN TOUR

"Things that we take for granted today would not have been possible then, and Shea Stadium cannot have been an impressive sonic experience. There were no purpose-built venues for music then."

MARTIN CLOONAN, Author and academic researching live music

Left: The adverse reaction to John's comments about the Beatles being more popular than Jesus was largely confined to the Bible belt. Popularity was unchanged in New York and homemade banners of support were displayed by fans at Shea Stadium.

IN THE EARLY MONTHS OF 1966, THE BEATLES WERE STILL AHEAD OF THE PACK, but they were facing fierce competition. The Rolling Stones and the Kinks were major acts in both Britain and America, and highly creative as well, and although they had yet to have U.S. hits, the Who were going to be a major force. American bands had bounced back with the Byrds, the Lovin' Spoonful, and the Beach Boys.

The Beach Boys' album, *Pet Sounds*, released in May 1966, was as adventurous as anything the Beatles had done. Most of that creativity was the work of one man—Brian Wilson—and his health was to suffer as he tried to match the Beatles.

Bob Dylan's double album, *Blonde on Blonde*, was released in May 1966. The combination of surreal lyrics with a rock beat was again unlike anything that had gone before.

The Beatles appeared in Tokyo for the first time in June 1966 and were very well received, but their performances were slapdash. The following month, in the Philippines, they appeared before eighty thousand fans at a football stadium in Manila, but they inadvertently snubbed an invitation from the president's wife, Imelda Marcos. There was enormously bad media coverage for the Beatles, though admittedly from a dictatorship, and even their security was withdrawn. They left the country in disgrace.

In August 1966 the Beatles released *Revolver*, an imaginative album with intriguing, often mystifying lyrics, ingenious arrangements, and testing melodies. Compared with this

Left: Arriving in triumph: the Beatles had no idea what was in store for them in the Philippines, but they came from a terrific reception in Tokyo and had huge ticket sales for their forthcoming Manila show.
Opposite: Leaving in disgrace: there was not much "free" about the *Philippines Free Press*, which was giving vent to Imelda Marcos' anger at being snubbed by the Beatles. (Note: the artefact is damaged and a patch at the bottom left corner repeats some text from the second column.)

effort, John Lennon thought of "She Loves You" as a nursery rhyme. When Bob Dylan heard the album, he said, "I get it. You don't want to be cute anymore."

The storm over John Lennon's comments about religion was erupting in the southern United States; this followed the furor over the first cover of *Yesterday and Today*. Back in London from their Tokyo trip, George Harrison said, "We're going to have a couple of weeks to recuperate before we go and get beaten up by the Americans."

Was George Harrison right? Would the Beatles be safe in America? Brian Epstein called the "bigger than Jesus" affair "a storm in a teacup," but, in truth, he was uneasy. Although he had influenza, he went to New York to reassure the fans, but also to give the individual promoters the opportunity to pull out of the forthcoming tour. He called it "taking care of business" (TCB), a term he had picked up from Colonel Parker. When Epstein was asked whether he thought that the Beatles were more popular than Jesus, he replied emphatically, "Of course not."

July 16, 1966

PHILIPPINES FREE PRESS

YEH YEH WAS THE RAPTUROUS CRY WHEN THEY ARRIVED

GO GO WAS THE ANGRY JEER WHEN THEY DEPARTED

From Yeh Yeh To Go Go

"I Don't Care What They Say I Won't Stay In A World Without Love!"

by Quijano de Manila

STAFF MEMBER

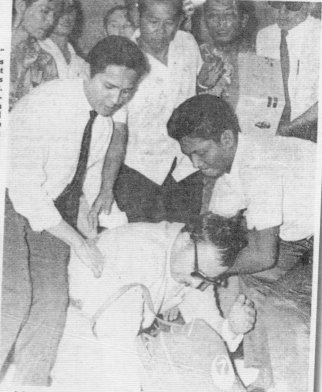

DOWN DOWN GOES A BEATLE MANAGER HIT BY THE MOB

THE SECOND British Invasion was as big a flop as the first.

The Mersey Sound, such a tonic in cans, proved a messy sound when fresh, and locally provoked a no-mercy sound.

Yeh, yeh, cried the four evangelists of beat. Go, go, snarled the locals — and they meant away, to hell, climb a tree, 'lis jan.

Well, at least, in this year of grace 1966, it wasn't the Yankees we were telling to go home on the Fourth of July.

The Grand and Glorious got stolen from the Stars and Stripes by the Union Jack, but the show it stole was not grand but inglorious.

Four boys had us on toast, had us on a string; we were had. Our whole society. From the Palace down. The constabulary and the police. The army, the navy and the marines. City Hall and the Fourth Estate. Not to mention Big Business.

Now we're all crying aghast that the Emperor had no clothes on. We're fooling ourselves again. The Emperor was dressed, it's we who were naked. We

so far "out" you become the most "in." They have reversed all the maxims. Does Mommy say you have to look clean-cut to get on in the world? So the Beatles wear their shags uncut and uncombed. Do the schoolma'ams teach that cleanliness is next to godliness? So the Beatles frankly stink. Are good manners and right conduct supposed to unlock the narrower doors of society? So the Beatles play the boor and won't go see a duchess if they don't feel like it. Is it considered

so far "out" you become the most "in." They have reversed all the maxims. Does Mommy say you have to look clean-cut to get on in the world? So the Beatles wear their shags uncut and uncombed. Do the schoolma'ams teach that cleanliness is next to godliness? So the Beatles frankly stink. Are good manners and right conduct supposed to unlock the narrower doors of society? So the Beatles play the boor and won't go see a duchess if they don't feel like it. Is it considered elegant to understate? So the Beatles go the whole hog, whether in music or attire.

By ignoring all the prescriptions to achieve status, they have achieved status. They have proved you don't have to be neat, clean, orderly, cultured, refined, holy or conventional to make a million, become an idol and get decorated by the Queen. Theirs is the triumph of the Outsider and their function in our time is to explode the bromides of the herd.

But Philippine society is an anxious status-seeker, especially in the world of Western mass culture. Whatever is "in" there, we would be with it. We are a conventional people, and even when we try to be unconventional it's for a very conventional reason: because "everybody's doing it." We would show ourselves as much "in" as any Westerner and our grasping at the latest fashions, the newest idioms, the hottest dances betrays our craving for cultural status in Western society. Now the kind of peo-

(Continued on page 33)

THE BEATLES THIRD
NORTH AMERICAN TOUR
August 12 to August 29, 1966

12 Seattle

6 Toronto

7 Boston

2 Detroit

11 New York

1 Chicago

3 Cleveland

5 Philadelphia

4 Washington

14 San Francisco

10 St. Louis

9 Cincinnati

8 Memphis

13 Los Angeles

01 International Ampitheater, Chicago, August 12, 1966

SHOWTIME 3 p.m. and 7:30 p.m.
ATTENDANCE 13,000 each show, sold out

02 Olympia Stadium, Detroit Saturday August 13, 1966

SHOWTIME 2 p.m. and 7 p.m.
ATTENDANCE 28,000 (total)

03 Cleveland Stadium, Cleveland Sunday August 14, 1966

SHOWTIME 7:30 p.m.
ATTENDANCE 20,000 **CAPACITY** Sold out

04 DC Stadium, Washington DC Monday August 15, 1966

SHOWTIME 8 p.m.
ATTENDANCE 32,164 **CAPACITY** Sold out

05 John F. Kennedy Stadium, Philadelphia, August 16, 1966

SHOWTIME 8 p.m.
ATTENDANCE 21,000 **CAPACITY** 64,000

06 Maple Leaf Gardens, Toronto Wednesday August 17, 1966

SHOWTIME 4 p.m. and 8 p.m.
ATTENDANCE 15,000 and 17,000

07 Suffolk Downs, Boston Thursday August 18, 1966

SHOWTIME 8 p.m.
ATTENDANCE 25,000

08 Mid-South Coliseum, Memphis Friday August 19, 1966

SHOWTIME 4 p.m. and 8:30 p.m.
ATTENDANCE 10,000 and 12,500

09 Crosley Field, Cincinnati Sunday August 21, 1966

SHOWTIME Noon.
ATTENDANCE 12,000 **CAPACITY** 15,000

10 Busch Stadium, St. Louis Sunday August 21, 1966

SHOWTIME 8:30 p.m.
ATTENDANCE 23,143 **CAPACITY** 40,000

11 Shea Stadium, New York City Tuesday August 23, 1966

SHOWTIME 7:30 p.m.
ATTENDANCE 44,600 **CAPACITY** 55,600

12 Coliseum, Seattle Thursday August 25, 1966

SHOWTIME 3 p.m. and 8 p.m.
ATTENDANCE 8,000 and 15,000

13 Dodgers Stadium, Los Angeles Sunday August 28, 1966

SHOWTIME 8 p.m.
ATTENDANCE 45,000 **CAPACITY** 56,000

14 Candlestick Park, San Francisco Monday August 29, 1966

SHOWTIME 8 p.m.
ATTENDANCE 25,000 **CAPACITY** 42,500

The only American act to be managed by Brian Epstein was a band called the Cyrkle, a misspelling like the Byrds; in fact, the name was suggested by John Lennon. They had had a U.S. hit with "Red Rubber Ball" in June 1966, and their new single was "Turn Down Day." They were booked to close the first half of the Beatles' 1966 U.S. tour; the remaining acts were the Ronettes, Bobby Hebb, and the Remains. The Remains would open the show and continue on stage to back Bobby Hebb, who had written "Sunny" to cheer himself up following his brother's death in a knife fight. The Ronettes, backed by the Remains, would open the second half, and then the Beatles would come on to close the show.

The Beatles performed the same set as in Japan and the Philippines: "Baby's in Black," "Day Tripper," "I Feel Fine," "I Wanna Be Your Man," "If I Needed Someone," "Nowhere Man," "Paperback Writer," "Rock and Roll Music," "She's a Woman," and "Yesterday," closing with "I'm Down," and later in the tour "Long Tall Sally." There was nothing from *Revolver*, an indication that they had done little rehearsing.

Above: Bobby Hebb's "Sunny" was by far his biggest hit. He set himself the task of writing a song a day, and one composition was "You Broke My Heart and I Broke Your Jaw."
Below: John Lennon changed the Rondells' name to Cyrkle. Their U.S. number two, "Red Rubber Ball" was written by Paul Simon with Bruce Woodley, from the Seekers.

BIGGER THAN ELVIS, BUT BIGGER THAN JESUS?

The Beatles were known for their off-the-wall comments, particularly in their famously jovial press conferences, but one such remark landed John in hot water in the U.S. in 1966.

IN MARCH 1966 A PROFILE OF JOHN LENNON by Maureen Cleave was published in the London *Evening Standard*. It had a clumsy title, "*How Does A Beatle Live? John Lennon Lives Like This,*" but it was candid and revelatory. Cleave knew John well, and her profile was unflattering, showing him to be listless and bored.

There was no mention of any drug habits, although that could easily be read into the text. The profile was about a celebrity who did not know what to do with his fame. One minute he was buying a gorilla suit; the next, an altar crucifix, a suit of armor, or model racing cars, but mostly he was lethargic, commenting, "I don't mind writing or reading or watching or speaking, but sex is the only physical thing I can be bothered with anymore."

One book among many that Lennon was dipping into at that time was *The Passover Plot* by an academic, Hugh J. Schonfield. Taking his lead from this book, John commented, "Christianity will go. It will vanish and shrink. I needn't argue about that; I'm right and I will be proved right. We're more popular than Jesus now; I don't know which will go first—rock 'n' roll or Christianity. Jesus was all right but his disciples were thick and ordinary. It's them twisting it that ruins it for me."

The problems began when the magazine, *Datebook*, printed John's comments out of context to imply that he was proud of the Beatles being bigger than Jesus. John admitted he was speaking lazily: "If I had said television is more popular than Jesus, I might have got away with it." The Bishop of Montreal, Kenneth Maguire, agreed with John. "I wouldn't be surprised if the Beatles actually were more popular than Jesus. In the only popularity poll in Jesus' lifetime, he came out second to Barabbas."

The complaints started with the radio station WAQY in Birmingham, Alabama, and spread around the Bible Belt southern states. Fans were asked to publicly destroy their Beatles' records and photographs. Paul laughed it off at first. "In order to burn the records, you've got to buy them, so it's no sweat off us, mate. It's not compulsory to play them." But as threats of repurcussions refused to go away, John was forced to apologize and to try to appear contrite—not his most natural look.

Above and right: Some of the protests against the Beatles were well-orchestrated affairs, borne out by the similar look and size of the placards above; burning photographs and records (right) looked dramatic, but the band brushed it off.

Opposite: This cartoon from the *Dallas Times Herald* in August 1966 takes a gentler approach, mocking John for his ill-advised remarks by showing him lifting his Beatles wig to reveal himself a pinhead (short on common sense) underneath.

STILL PLEASED TO MEET YOU?

The Beatles found the shows a chore on this third American tour, no longer a pleasure or an exhilarating buzz—one indication of this was the quicker tempo at which they played, completing eleven songs within thirty minutes as if they couldn't wait to get off the stage. Elvis, who was no longer performing, had rarely performed any longer on stage, but their loyal fans could be forgiven for feeling a little bit cheated. Even the easygoing Ringo was disillusioned: "I had wanted to join the Beatles because they were the best band in Liverpool. That was OK at the beginning, but it got that we were playing really bad."

George was right to be apprehensive about the month ahead of them. This was to be a tour of fear, foul-ups, and lots of

Above: Apologizing for anything did not come easy to any of the Beatles and at their Chicago press conference, despite Brian Epstein's instructions, John was reluctant to simply say, "I'm sorry" for the offense he caused with his "bigger than Jesus" comment. He should have been a politician!

rain. Fans at the airport in London had screamed, "Don't go, John. They'll kill you." Potentially true, but there is also a fine line between hysteria and violence, and even the loyal fans could kill you. Robert Whitaker commented, "There was a constant threat of violence around the Beatles. If their fans had got hold of them, they would have been torn to pieces."

The Beatles were continually asked if their popularity was fading, because often the stadiums were not sold out. However, they were still performing to huge audiences, and if they had instigated today's practice of calling it the "Final Tour", they would have sold every seat.

Below: The Beatles had fan clubs all over America, producing regular bulletins like this one. The band members would often meet the local fan club secretaries when they visited a city.
Bottom: Bill Hanley manning the mixing decks at the Woodstock Festival in 1969. The Beatles were impressed with his sound set-up for the Remains on this tour.

International Ampitheater, Chicago
Friday August 12, 1966

SHOWTIME 3 p.m. and 7:30 p.m.
ATTENDANCE 13,000 each show
CAPACITY Sold out

The Beatles arrived in Chicago at 4:15 p.m. and there was a press conference at the Astor Hotel, which was broadcast nationally. Their jokey affability had gone; this was a serious affair, with the Beatles battling for credibility and it was clear that John Lennon had been crying before the conference.

Brian Epstein had told John Lennon to say "Sorry" for his comments about the band being bigger than Jesus, which had caused such a furor. Looking pale and wan, he said, in a half-hearted way, "If you want me to apologize, if that will make you happy, then I'm sorry." Ringo was silent; when asked to contribute, he said, "Well, I just hope it's all over now, you know, everything's straightened out and it's finished."

For the tour, Bill Hanley of Hanley Sound had developed a stadium sound system for the Remains, and Brian Epstein was impressed. This was the first concert sound company in the U.S. and Hanley would famously go on to design the sound system at the Woodstock Festival in 1969. As the Remains' kit was clearly better than the Beatles', they were asked to let the Beatles use their sound equipment for most of the remaining shows, so on this tour—at last—perhaps the fans would be able to hear them playing.

Don Dannemann of the Cyrkle commented on the tour's opening night, "The first night we wondered if the fans would boo us off the stage and demand the Beatles, but they whooped and hollered and we did well." Red rubber balls had been handed out to promote the Cyrkle, and the fans held onto them while they performed. They threw them at the Beatles—along with jelly beans, of course.

The wires for the amplifiers in the Amphitheater ran along the balcony on both sides of the stage. When some fans were dancing, they kicked loose the plug to the power supply. Fortunately Mal Evans realized what had happened and quickly sorted it out, restoring the sound.

Above: The Chicago concert is recorded as having been a sell-out, but this photograph shows rows of empty seats behind the stage. Perhaps the venue chose not to sell tickets for seats behind the band for reasons of security?
Right: The Beatles were in good company in the list of acts playing the Chicago "Summer of Stars."
Opposite top: The limousine taking the Beatles to their Chicago motel was mobbed by fans. Some of them even clambered onto the trunk of the moving vehicle in an effort to see inside.
Opposite below: George had been learning to play sitar: here the rest of the band looks on while he takes a lesson from a Sikh teacher in New Delhi in July 1966, just before their U.S. tour.

TRIANGLE THEATRICAL PRODUCTIONS, INC.
FRANKLIN FRIED, EXECUTIVE DIRECTOR
PRESENTS
SUMMER OF STARS '66
THE SECOND ANNUAL
SUMMER OF STARS
IN CHICAGO

TONY BENNETT & WOODY HERMAN June 24 & 25 — $6.50, $5.50, $4.50, $3.50
PAUL REVERE AND THE RAIDERS .... July 2 — $5.50, $4.50, $3.50, $2.50
THE ROLLING STONES July 10 — at 3:30 and 7:30 P.M. — $6.50, $5.50, $4.50, $3.50
FOLK FESTIVAL: JUDY COLLINS, THE MITCHELL TRIO,
TOM PAXTON, STAPLE SINGERS .... July 15 — $5.50, $4.50, $3.50, $2.50
THE BEACHBOYS .... July, 16, 17 & 18 — $5.50, $4.50, $3.50, $2.50
THE BYRDS .... July 20 — $5.50, $4.50, $3.50, $2.50
ANDY WILLIAMS & HENRY MANCINI ...July 22 & 23 — Two Shows Daily
9:00 P. M. — $7.50, $6.50, $5.50, $4.50
6:00 P. M. — $6.50, $5.50, $4.50, $3.50
SKITCH HENDERSON & NORM CROSBY July 30 — $5.50, $4.50, $3.50, $2.50
SIMON & GARFUNKEL .... July 31 — $5.50, $4.50, $3.50, $2.50
PETER NERO & THE YOUNG AMERICANS August 5 — $5.50, $4.50, $3.50, $2.50
THE KINGSTON TRIO .... August 6 — $5.50, $4.50, $3.50, $2.50
THE BEATLES—INTERNATIONAL AMPHITHEATRE
August 12 — 3:00 & 7:30 P.M. — $5.75, $4.75, $3.75
BILL COSBY & CHAD MITCHELL ......August 13 — $6.50, $5.50, $4.50, $3.50
THE NEW CHRISTY MINSTRELS & THE DAVE BRUBECK QUARTET
August 14 — $5.50, $4.50, $3.50, $2.50
JERRY VALE .... August 21 — $5.50, $4.50, $3.50, $2.50
PETER, PAUL & MARY .... August 27 & 28 — $5.50, $4.50, $3.50, $2.50
All Attractions at Arie Crown Theatre—McCormick Place
23rd STREET AND LAKE SHORE DRIVE, CHICAGO, ILLINOIS
TO ORDER TICKETS SEND A CHECK OR MONEY ORDER TO TRIANGLE PRODUCTIONS,
211 E. CHICAGO AVENUE, CHICAGO, ILLINOIS 60611.
ENCLOSE A SELF-ADDRESSED STAMPED ENVELOPE AND 25c PER ORDER FOR HANDLING.

The screaming for the Beatles was as intense as ever, but they were quiet when Paul sang "Yesterday." Audiences would go "Shhh" as George introduced Paul. If the Beatles had continued touring, they might have gotten the fans to be silent for other numbers as well.

In a sign of the times, George had brought along instruction cassettes for playing the sitar by Ravi Shankar, practicing in hotel rooms during the tour.

continued on page 180

TEENAGE MAGAZINES

Even in the 1960s, most teenage girls wanted an insight into the celebrity world that good newspapers did not give. Magazines aimed just at them had a vast and enthusiastic market.

THE BEATLES WERE FAMILIAR WITH THE BRITISH PRESS. The quality newspapers were disdainful of popular music; for instance, in February 1959, the *Times* did not even mention the death of Buddy Holly. The tabloid papers included lighthearted features about pop stars, and in 1963 they seized the initiative by running daily stories on the Beatles and other contemporary performers.

The weekly music press, led by *New Musical Express* and *Melody Maker*, printed interviews and friendly gossip, with little investigative reporting: for example, they ran nothing but favorable reports about the highly troubled Gene Vincent. There were magazines for teenage girls, such as *Fab*, and the romance comic strips *Valentine* and *Roxy*.

In 1963 the monthly publication *The Beatles Book*, which was endorsed by Brian Epstein, appealed to a niche market of super-fans who were given insider information and exclusive photographs. At the time, *The Beatles Book* was dismissed by serious music fans, but now it can be seen to provide a superb cultural history of the group.

The U.S. scene differed from the United Kingdom, as its music papers, *Billboard* and *Cashbox*, although available nationally, were mainly produced for the trade. There was a range of exposé magazines, usually focused on sex and scandal, such as the *National Enquirer* and *True Confessions,* and these carried stories about celebrity lives and news. At one press conference, John Lennon commented on the scurrilous stories that he saw in the confession magazines: "In England, they wouldn't be allowed to write the things they write here."

Left: Sack the artist! The girls on the front cover of this issue of *Laugh* are clearly dreaming of the Beatles, but the drawings could have been much better.
Opposite: A typical example of *16*'s tie-in with the Beatles. Publishing information about "Where they'll stay in the U.S." was asking for trouble.

BEATLES

50c

16 SCOOP!

100

WHOLE TRUE STORY

7 GIGANTIC COLOR PIN-UPS

HOT NEVER-BEFORE-SEEN PIX

WHERE THEY'LL STAY IN THE U.S. ● TOUR & TICKET INFO ● HOW YOU CAN MEET THEM !

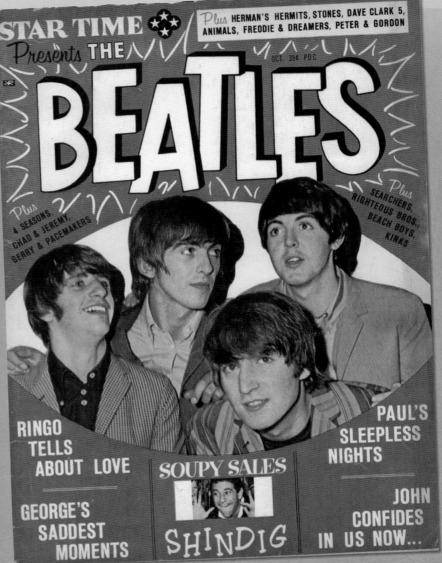

Girls wanted the gossip, but without the sleaze. The U.S. magazine *16* was founded in 1956; the title referred to its target audience. *16* carried features about dream dates, such as the good-looking, well-dressed pop singers of the early '60s. There were photographs of the performers at home and with their families. Strangely, none of these fellows seemed to have permanent girlfriends, and they were always looking for someone—the inference being that that "someone" could be *you*. The readers could imagine romantic evenings with Paul Anka, Ricky Nelson, and Bobby Rydell, all ending with a kiss at the doorstep. The readers would know what to wear, as the singers (or their press agents) described what they looked for in a girl and what colors they favored. The ultimate bachelor boy was Elvis Presley, but the true extent of his partying was not revealed.

In 1958, the editor of *16* was a feisty thirty-two-year-old former model, Gloria Stavers. She was always looking for ways to boost circulation, especially as there were rival publications. She had to be up to date and correctly predict what would happen next or she might lose some of her million readers. When Brian Epstein first went to New York with Billy J. Kramer, his press officer Tony Barrow advised him to contact Stavers at her Park Avenue office. Barrow realized the importance of *16* in breaking an act. The Beatles were strongly featured in *16* from January 1964 onwards, and when they first met Stavers, she said, "Hi, I'm *16*"—to which Ringo retorted, "You don't look sixteen: you look much younger."

Unlike other subjects in *16*, John Lennon was known to be married, but Stavers and Barrow resolved this issue brilliantly. *16* would give the Beatles' partners some status; they would be featured in their own right. Each month George's wife, Pattie Boyd, a former model with an impressive knowledge of current fashions, wrote a column from Swinging London. Jane Asher was featured in color, and when the magazine introduced Peter and Gordon, the headline was Peter's quote, "Paul's my best mate," which may have needled Gordon.

The Rolling Stones were the obvious rivals to the Beatles, but Stavers was reluctant to push a Beatles versus Stones agenda because the latter were rough-edged and badly dressed. One feature was "The Rolling Stones—Has England gone too far?" "Five against four isn't fair," commented George Harrison. The Stones were featured from time to time, but largely because Stavers realized Brian Jones looked perfect.

Purely on looks, the Dave Clark Five were promoted as the main rival to the Beatles, which tied in with Ed Sullivan, as he featured the Five on his show eighteen times. Herman's Hermits had the same double benefit, and their young lead singer, Peter Noone, was exceptionally savvy about the value of publicity. He

BEATLES
COMPLETE STORY FROM BIRTH TO NOW
16 SCOOP!
7 HUGE COLOR PIN-UPS · OVER 100 HOT NEW PIX

35¢

HOME ADDRESSES PERSONAL AUTOGRAPHS

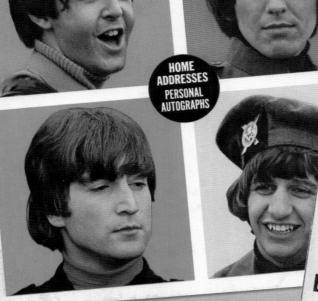

Opposite: The U.S. comedian Soupy Sales was a great hit with adolescents and had his own hit single with a dance record, "The Mouse." *Shindig* was a beat show featuring live music and directed by the British producer, Jack Good.
Left and below: The fans' appetite for Beatles stories, pictures, posters, and "insider secrets" was insatiable.

AMERICA'S FINEST TEENAGE MAGAZINE

teen talk

VALUABLE COLLECTOR'S EDITION ON

THE BEATLES
PICTURE-PACKED EDITION ON THEIR VISIT TO U.S.A.

PLUS Intimate Interviews with each BEATLEBOY

Exclusive Photos - Intimate Secrets
FULL PAGES OF PICTURES SUITABLE FOR FRAMING

remained a friend of Stavers and was at her bedside when she died in 1983.

When the Beatles stopped being cute, Stavers promoted the Monkees. She did take the magazine into psychedelia and featured such controversial figures as Jim Morrison (with the Doors) and Janis Joplin. For a long time, the magazine did not feature black artists. Even though the Supremes had a succession of number one records, they were hardly mentioned in *16*. In fact, the magazine did not deal with black artists until the Jackson Five.

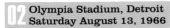

02 Olympia Stadium, Detroit
Saturday August 13, 1966

SHOWTIME 2 p.m. and 7 p.m.

ATTENDANCE 28,000 (total)

CAPACITY 30,000 (total)

The Beatles arrived at 11 a.m. on their return visit to Detroit, and as Beatle concerts go, these two were uneventful. The police kept the fans under control, and the Beatles listened to Indian music before they went on stage. The Beatles left by Greyhound bus for Cleveland directly after the show. Along the way, they stopped at a roadside café for hamburgers.

Although all was normal in the North, the Beatles were apprehensive about the South. Station KLUE in Longview, Texas, had been the first to criticize the Beatles, and DJs announced that Saturday night was bonfire night. Alternatively, fans could break or pulverize the records—another radio station made a wood chipper available.

03 Cleveland Stadium, Cleveland
Sunday August 14, 1966

SHOWTIME 7:30 p.m.

ATTENDANCE 20,000 **CAPACITY** Sold out

Originally, the Beatles had been scheduled to play a concert on this tour in Louisville, Kentucky, but the venue was switched to Cleveland. After the unruly crowd problems during the 1964 concert there, a ban had been imposed on the Beatles' performing again in Cleveland, but a promoter persuaded the authorities to change their mind, and the band was permitted to return. This time they were to perform in a baseball stadium, the home of the Cleveland Indians. They arrived at 2:30 a.m. in heavy rain, but although the stadium did not have a roof, the stage was covered.

The city apparently hadn't learned by experience, because although there was a large police presence. much of the policing was done by volunteers. The Beatles performed on a stage five feet high, but two thousand fans broke through the barrier and the police line, and charged the stage during "Day Tripper." The Beatles later would say that it was the best reaction to "Day Tripper" they'd ever had.

The concert was stopped and the Beatles retreated to their trailer. There was no refuge there, and it was soon surrounded by fans, who even climbed onto the roof. The fans were told that the concert would not continue if they didn't sit down, but after thirty minutes the performance did resume.

At the end, the fans surged forward again, some trying to take the instruments for souvenirs, but roadie Mal Evans managed to rescue them intact.

During the evening, radio station KLUE in Longview, Texas—which had called for Beatle records to be burned—was hit by lightning, ruining some equipment, taking it off the air, and knocking the news director unconscious. Could this have been divine intervention?

Right: The concert in Cleveland had to be stopped temporarily after two thousand fans stormed the stage during the Beatles' set (a fan captured the confusion, but you can see the band valiantly trying to play on). For the police charged with controlling the audience it must have been a night's work they would always remember. Many of the police that night were volunteer helpers and not trained in this kind of crowd control.

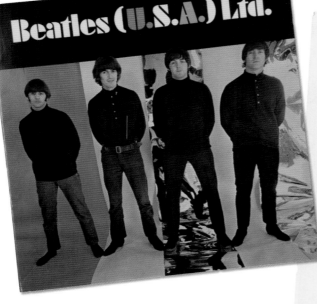

Above: Each tour was accompanied by a program. This one from 1966 shows the band in a sober pose: in fact they preferred more serious shots to the "larking about" images publicists so often used.

Bottom and Right: A ticket and official parking permit for the August 16 concert at Philadelphia's John F. Kennedy Stadium.

Opposite page: A playful shot of Alf Bicknell (left) and Mal Evans, two of Brian Epstein's team, who made sure that the tour ran smoothly. Alf Bicknell was the band's driver, but became a more integral part of the team than that implies. He wrote his memoirs (twice!) to record his experiences on tour with the Beatles.

PRESENTED AT
JOHN F. KENNEDY STADIUM
PHILA., PA.
AUG. 16, 1966
8:00 P.M.
UNDER AUSPICES
STEEL PIER
MANAGEMENT
EST. PRICE $4.76
CITY TAX .24
TOTAL $5.00
GLOBE TICKET COMPANY, PHILA.
ADMIT ONE $5.00
Sec. 11 Row N ED
BEATLES $5.00

CITY LICENSE FEE PER CAR ....$ .10
CITY PARKING TAX .... .10
REMITTANCE TO CITY
PARKING CHARGE ....$ .20
.80
COST OF PARKING TICKET $1.00

★ ★ ☆ ★ ★

NOT RESPONSIBLE FOR THEFT OR DAMAGE CAR OR CONTENTS

№ 881

OFFICIAL PARKING
$1.00 AUGUST 16, 196
The
BEATLES'

LOCK CAR — REMOVE VALUABLES — TAKE KEYS

HANG THIS TICKET ON INSIDE REAR VIEW MIRROR

Beatles (U.S.A.) Ltd.

**04 DC Stadium, Washington DC
Monday August 15, 1966**

SHOWTIME 8 p.m.

ATTENDANCE 32,164 **CAPACITY** Sold out

**06 Maple Leaf Gardens, Toronto
Wednesday August 17, 1966**

SHOWTIME 4 p.m. and 8 p.m.

ATTENDANCE 15,000 and 17,000

CAPACITY 17,766

The notorious Ku Klux Klan had joined the attack on the Beatles; they claimed that they were a religious organization and, as such, they were legitimately objecting to John Lennon's comments about Christianity, notwithstanding his apology, made in Chicago.

A contingent from the Maryland KKK showed up outside the DC Stadium—the home field of the Washington Senators—in their white robes and hoods, urging fans to not go in to the concert and to destroy their Beatles records. There was a huge police presence, but violence didn't erupt. Still, this was the first indication of bad vibes at a concert, and the Beatles had yet to go into the Deep South.

**05 John F. Kennedy Stadium,
Philadelphia, August 16, 1966**

SHOWTIME 8 p.m.

ATTENDANCE 21,000 **CAPACITY** 64,000

In terms of ticket sales, the Philadelphia concert was a disappointment. An audience of twenty-one thousand is excellent, and few other bands would have had that pulling power, but with a capacity of sixty-four thousand, the venue wasn't even half full. Just before entering the stadium, the Beatles switched from the tour bus to a delivery van belonging to a local florist.

This was an open-air concert in bad weather. There was lightning, and a storm threatened to disrupt the concert at any moment. When Paul announced "Long Tall Sally," he said it was the last song, as he didn't want to be struck by lightning. Ten minutes after the show finished, there was a heavy downpour. The Beatles were taken by Greyhound to the airport for their flight to Canada.

Brian Epstein had told the Beatles that they must not comment on Vietnam, but even after the trouble over religion, there was no stopping John Lennon. At the press conference at Toronto's King Edward Sheraton Hotel, John encouraged Americans to move to Canada to avoid the draft and expressed admiration for those who had already done so. There were mixed feelings over the war—the right-wing "Ballad of the Green Berets" by S/Sgt Barry Sadler had been RCA's fastest-selling single. The FBI was concerned that a band that attracted as much attention as the Beatles might quite easily become a very influential voice for the anti-war movement.

Four hundred policemen were on duty at this concert, but even so a pair of scissors was thrown by a member of the audience—presumably as a joke on account of the Beatles' "long" hair—and narrowly missed Paul's head.

TOO MUCH MONKEE BUSINESS

In 1965, two young film producers, Bob Rafelson and Bert Schneider, noticed that the Beatles were outgrowing their young fans, leaving a potential gap in the market.

THEY HAD BEEN CAPTIVATED BY THE ZANINESS of the Beatles' film, *A Hard Day's Night*, and wanted a four-man group for a similarly energetic half-hour TV series that would capture the zeitgeist. At first they thought of the Lovin' Spoonful, but they quickly decided it would be better to create their own group.

They ran an ad in the *Hollywood Reporter* in September 1965, announcing auditions for a new TV series with "running parts for 4 insane boys, aged 17–21." As a result, 437 hopefuls were auditioned by Rafelson and Schneider. Stephen Stills, Danny Hutton (later with Three Dog Night), composer Paul Williams, and future mass murderer Charles Manson were rejected (and found fame or notoriety elsewhere).

The successful applicants were Davy Jones (the Artful Dodger in *Oliver!* on Broadway), Mickey Dolenz (the child star of the TV series *Circus Boy* and a competent drummer and singer), Mike Nesmith (a singer-songwriter working in folk music), and Peter Tork (a singer and guitarist who had opened for José Feliciano). The group was named the Monkees, possibly

because they aped the Beatles. However, they could never fully be America's answer to the Beatles, as Davy Jones was British.

The Monkees' songs were all commissioned from Screen Gems—a smart choice, as their writers included Gerry Goffin and Carole King, Neil Sedaka and Howard Greenfield, and Tommy Boyce and Bobby Hart. The music would be recorded by top session men, and the Monkees themselves would simply add their voices in the studio.

NBC launched *The Monkees* on September 12, 1966, just four days after the start of another new series, *Star Trek*. Even on the theme song, the Monkees sang "no, no, no"—a counterpoint to the Beatles' "yeah, yeah, yeah."

Their first single, "Last Train to Clarksville," was a close cousin to "Paperback Writer." Then followed "I'm a Believer," written by the up-and-coming Neil Diamond. Mike Nesmith, probably being contrary at his own songwriting talents being overlooked, would have nothing to do with it—"I'm a songwriter," he told

Left: People say we monkey around: the Monkees had a different escapade each week in their television series. **Above right:** Davy and Mickey were showbiz types who willingly did whatever was required. Pete went along for the ride, but Mike was always questioning and was the one who insisted they play on their records.

the producer Jeff Barry, "and that's no hit." Barry wouldn't stand for this insolence and banned him from the studio, leaving Mickey Dolenz to take the lead vocal. The song topped the U.S. charts for seven weeks.

Brian Epstein presented the Monkees at the Empire Pool, Wembley for four days from June 30, 1967. The Beatles were among the guests at a party at the Speakeasy, and befriended the individual Monkees, inviting them to their homes and recording sessions. Peter Tork eventually played banjo on George Harrison's soundtrack for the film *Wonderwall*.

The Monkees were hurt by press comments that they did not play their instruments, and, encouraged by Mike Nesmith, they insisted on playing on their third album, *Headquarters*, which included many of their own songs. "Randy Scouse Git," written by Mickey Dolenz, referred to "the four kings of EMI." Their next album, *The Birds, the Bees and the Monkees*, included their best performance, John Stewart's "Daydream Believer."

After fifty-eight episodes, their TV series ended in March 1968. The Monkees had their *Magical Mystery Tour* moment with the film *Head*, which featured Frank Zappa and probably made sense only to Zappa fans. If the intention had been to break the Monkees' mold, then the producers were very successful.

Michael (no longer known as Mike) had by far the most creative musical career after they split—"Joanne," "Silver Moon," "Rio"—but the responsibility of managing his inheritance (his mother invented Liquid Paper) meant that he has only recorded and performed sporadically.

Peter Tork says, "Of course I wouldn't stack our albums against the Beatles or the Stones one to one. I don't think we had anything quite as good as 'California Dreamin'' or 'Monday, Monday,' but we have three hours' worth of songs, and Mr. and Mrs. America and Mr. and Mrs. Great Britain know a lot of them. Have you seen the mashup on *YouTube*? Somebody has taken out our vocals to 'I'm A Believer' and put in the Beatles' vocals to 'Paperback Writer.' They have blended our videos together, and it's great."

185

07 Suffolk Downs, Boston
Thursday August 18, 1966

SHOWTIME 8 p.m.
ATTENDANCE 25,000

The Boston concert was originally going to be in Fenway Park, but it was switched to a racetrack, with the Beatles performing on the central green. Mounted police kept fans away from the band. During the Remains' set, one of the amps blew a fuse. Fortunately, the Vox rep was around and able to fix it for the Beatles before they came on to play. The Beatles stayed at a local hotel and left for Memphis the following morning.

08 Mid-South Coliseum, Memphis
Friday August 19, 1966

SHOWTIME 4 p.m. and 8:30 p.m.
ATTENDANCE 10,000 and 12,500
CAPACITY 13,300

Early in 1966 there had been talk of the Beatles recording some of the tracks for *Revolver* in Memphis, but it would have been time-consuming and costly. Paul said, "We wanted to come. A couple of tracks would have been much better if we had come. We wanted Steve Cropper, the guitarist for Booker T. & the MG's, to A&R the session. He's the best we've heard."

Now, heading south en route to Memphis, the feeling was not so positive. When John was asked how he was feeling, he replied, "Ask me again after Memphis." That was hardly surprising, as a member of the Ku Klux Klan had said in an interview: "The Beatles said that they were better than Jesus himself, and the Ku Klux Klan, being a religious order, is going to come out here when they play at the Coliseum. I shall have about fifty men in robes and quite a few inside the stadium." A local preacher, Reverend Jimmy Stroad, urged fans not to attend this concert, and he fronted a peaceful protest of one hundred fundamentalist ministers.

It may have been nothing to do with the KKK, but in the second show, during "If I Needed Someone" someone threw a cherry bomb. Tony Barrow recalls, "I was standing in the wings at the concert and the worst moment was when a firecracker exploded in the audience. Each of the Beatles glanced at the others to see if one of them would drop. It says something for them that they didn't miss a note."

In an interview in 1968, John and Paul were asked about the highlight of their three American tours, and John replied, "Escaping from Memphis!"

09 Crosley Field, Cincinnati
Sunday August 21, 1966

SHOWTIME Noon
ATTENDANCE 12,000 **CAPACITY** 15,000

In Cincinnati, the bandstand, with its canvas top, was in the middle of the ballpark at Crosley Field. The promoter was trying to save money by not having a suitable roof for the stage, and he hadn't appreciated the fact that the Beatles played electric instruments. Fortunately for him, he did have a rain check clause in his contract for the event, permitting the concert to be carried over to the next day in the event of bad weather.

The concert was originally scheduled for Saturday, August 20, at 8:30 p.m. The fans had arrived and were all in their seats, and it was agreed that the concert would go ahead as planned, despite the threatening weather.

Just before the Beatles were to appear, though, there was a ferocious downpour. While connecting the Beatles' amplifiers, Mal Evans received a shock and was thrown across the stage. The Beatles decided not to perform; instead, they would appear the next day. Fifteen thousand fans were sent home, and twelve thousand of them returned in the morning for a show that started at noon. It had stopped raining, and the Beatles performed for half an hour. Then they had to fly 340 miles to Missouri for an evening performance that same day.

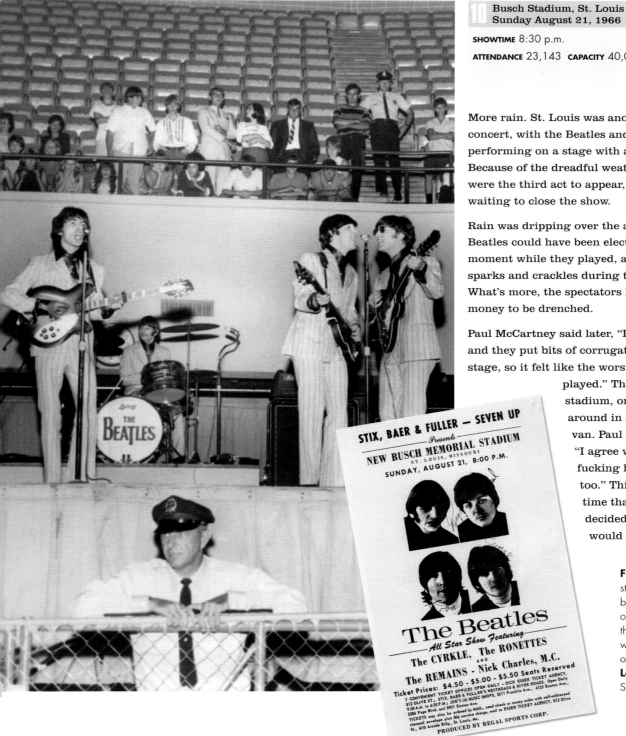

10 Busch Stadium, St. Louis
Sunday August 21, 1966

SHOWTIME 8:30 p.m.

ATTENDANCE 23,143 **CAPACITY** 40,000

More rain. St. Louis was another open-air concert, with the Beatles and support acts performing on a stage with a tarpaulin cover. Because of the dreadful weather, the Beatles were the third act to appear, rather than waiting to close the show.

Rain was dripping over the amplifiers, so the Beatles could have been electrocuted at any moment while they played, and there were sparks and crackles during their performance. What's more, the spectators had paid good money to be drenched.

Paul McCartney said later, "It rained heavily, and they put bits of corrugated iron over the stage, so it felt like the worst gig we'd ever played." The Beatles left the stadium, only to be tossed around in an empty removals van. Paul said to the others, "I agree with you. I've fucking had it up to here too." This was the first time that all four Beatles decided that the touring would stop.

Far left: The Beatles on stage in Memphis. The band feared protests—or even attack—from the Ku Klux Klan and were relieved to get out of town.
Left: A poster for the St Louis concert.

STIX, BAER & FULLER — SEVEN UP
Presents
NEW BUSCH MEMORIAL STADIUM
ST. LOUIS, MISSOURI
SUNDAY, AUGUST 21, 8:00 P.M.

The Beatles
All Star Show Featuring
The CYRKLE, The RONETTES
AND
The REMAINS - Nick Charles, M.C.
Ticket Prices: $4.50 - $5.00 - $5.50 Seats Reserved
7 CONVENIENT TICKET OFFICES OPEN DAILY — DICK ESSER TICKET AGENCY,
812 OLIVE ST.; STIX, BAER & FULLER'S WESTROADS & RIVER ROADS. Open Daily
9:30 A.M. to 4:30 P.M.; JOE'S (4) MUSIC SHOPS, 2611 Franklin Ave., 4123 Easton Ave.,
5286 Page Blvd. and 5901 Easton Ave.
TICKETS may also be ordered by MAIL, send check or money order with self-addressed
stamped envelope plus 50¢ service charge, mail to ESSER TICKET AGENCY, 812 Olive
St., W10 Arcade Bldg., St. Louis, Mo.
PRODUCED BY REGAL SPORTS CORP.

Above: The merchandising of the band continued: with packets of Lux Beauty Soap eager fans could purchase their very own autographed, inflatable Beatles for just two wrappers and $2.00. Button badges were cheap enough for even the youngest fan.

Right: Fantastic hair! Police stop a fan from trying to break through the barriers.

11 Shea Stadium, New York City
Tuesday August 23, 1966

SHOWTIME 7:30 p.m.
ATTENDANCE 44,600 **CAPACITY** 55,600

On August 22, the Beatles had free time at the Warwick Hotel in New York City. Two press conferences were arranged at the Warwick: one for journalists, and one for seventy-five fans chosen by the radio station WMCA. Just before the main press conference, Tony Barrow said, "The Beatles are about to enter. I'd like to ask the people in front to kneel." This got a big laugh.

During the second conference, the Dronge family, makers of Guild guitars, gave Lennon a customized Guild Starfire XII electric twelve-string guitar. When Mark Dronge brought the guitar into the room, George thought it was for him, but Mark gave it to John. Lennon later gave the guitar to Tony Cox, the former husband of Yoko Ono; he eventually sold it to the Hard Rock Café in Honolulu.

Few Beatles concerts passed without incident, and this one was no exception. Two girls on the twenty-second storey of a nearby building threatened to jump if the Beatles did not visit them, but they were talked down. Then the promoter Sid Bernstein gave the Beatles a large cake, but on learning that it didn't contain a scantily clad woman, John said, "We don't want your fucking cake."

The Beatles performed well, but their sound couldn't compete with the screaming. During "Day Tripper"— why was it always that song?—hundreds of fans broke through the barriers and attempted to reach the stage. They were held back by the security guards.

Unlike 1965, this concert was not sold out, although forty-five thousand is a respectable turnout. Sid Bernstein did try to book the Beatles for Shea in 1967, but they had had enough. This time the Beatles were playing for 65 percent of the take of $292,000, roughly $190,000, so despite the smaller audience, they made more money.

The last word on Shea Stadium can go to Brenda Holloway, the concert's opening act: "I am so happy that I did that. There were a lot of things going on racially when I started, but I had a lot of opportunities for a black woman. It was wonderful to be able to perform with the Beatles and to be accepted by them and everyone else."

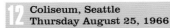

Coliseum, Seattle
Thursday August 25, 1966

SHOWTIME 3 p.m. and 8 p.m.

ATTENDANCE 8,000 and 15,000

CAPACITY 15,000

From New York, the band headed to Hollywood. The Beatles went to the Capitol Records Tower for a press conference on August 24, after which they were given a gold disc for *Revolver*.

Paul was asked about contemporary bands stealing from them; he replied, "We pinch as much from other people as they pinch from us." Most of the time they couldn't muster the wit of past tours, but fell back on bored, flippant answers. One typical exchange went like this: "What was the inspiration for 'Eleanor Rigby'?" "Two queers."

The Beatles left Hollywood to play afternoon and evening shows in Seattle the following day and they stayed at the

Edgewater Inn, in Seattle. It was rumored that Jane Asher was flying in and she and Paul were going to be married in Seattle—a rumor that Paul played along with for a while.

After the show, they went straight to the airport to fly to Los Angeles, but they had to wait as the plane needed a new tire.

Dodgers Stadium, Los Angeles
Sunday August 28, 1966

SHOWTIME 8 p.m.

ATTENDANCE 45,000 **CAPACITY** 56,000

While the Dodgers were playing the Giants in San Francisco, the Beatles were playing the first concert in the Dodgers' four-year-old stadium. The Beatles would be playing on the Giants' home field the next day. There was a fence around the field, and the Beatles performed on a raised stage placed over second base. The Beatles were brought to the stadium

in an armored car that parked behind the stage. During the performance someone deflated the tires.

The promoter Bob Eubanks had presented the Beatles in 1964 and 1965, too. He noticed a change in the band over the years: "The first year, McCartney and Harrison were very friendly. The second year, McCartney was real friendly, and in the third year, they were a pain. I forgave them because they were tired. They were tired of their own music, and they were tired of each other. They had had enough."

Even if the Beatles never said "Goodnight," everybody in the audience knew that "Long Tall Sally" was the closing song, and as soon as they heard it, they rushed toward the stage. Police used clubs, and the crowd wielded

Above: When the Beatles came to Seattle, the local newspaper the *Seattle Post-Intelligencer* produced a souvenir edition, devoting the entire front cover to news about the band.
Left: Setting the template for today's rock bands, the Beatles on stage at Shea Stadium, on August 23, 1966.

wooden barricades. Bottles and sticks were thrown, and there were many injuries and broken bones.

The Beatles rushed off stage to a limousine, but by the time the car reached the entrance, fans were everywhere, and the driver had to reverse. Fortunately, no one was seriously injured. The driver headed for a dugout at the far end of the stadium and the Beatles were imprisoned for two hours in a dressing room. John Lennon was unhappy, as he had made other plans, but the tension was eased when Ringo said plaintively, "Can I please go home to my mummy now?"

KEY CONCERT: CANDLESTICK PARK

14 **Candlestick Park, San Francisco**
Monday August 29, 1966

SHOWTIME 8 p.m.

ATTENDANCE 25,000 **CAPACITY** 42,500

There was an end-of-term feeling to this San Francisco concert, as—although nothing had been announced—the Beatles knew this would be their last performance, certainly in stadiums in America.

THE VENUE WAS NOT SOLD OUT; STILL, THERE WERE TWENTY-FIVE THOUSAND FANS, and the Beatles had difficulty in getting onto the field; their vehicles had to circle around like real-life bumper cars until they could find a way through. While they waited to go on stage, they had a jam session with Joan Baez in their dressing room.

The stage, positioned on second base just like at the Dodgers' stadium the previous night, was five feet above the ground and surrounded by a six-foot wire fence. In front of the stage were two hundred police and security men. It was August, and a typically cold, foggy, and windy summer night in San Francisco; still, Bobby Hebb sang "Sunny." Macca said, "Thank you very much, everybody. We'd like to say that it's been wonderful being here in this wonderful sea air."

Paul McCartney asked Tony Barrow to tape the show on his portable cassette recorder. Barrow did so with a C60 cassette. The recording, which has been bootlegged, runs out after thirty minutes as the Beatles were still performing "Long Tall Sally." The fact that McCartney wanted a recording suggests that it would be their last show, and he wanted to keep it for posterity. Their tiredness is often apparent in their performance. George was having trouble with the high harmonies on "Paperback Writer," and there is no sparkle to "If I Needed Someone." Ringo couldn't even remember the second verse of "I Wanna Be Your Man."

The Beatles had fun with their introductions. John said, "This is about a naughty lady called Day Tripper." He was also, very unprofessionally, taking photos of the others on stage. Just before "Long Tall Sally," they turned their backs to the audience, and Mal Evans took a wide shot with the audience behind them. This photograph has never been released publicly.

NOT A BEATLE ANY MORE

"Long Tall Sally" was an appropriate closer particularly for this concert, as it goes back to the band's earliest days. Paul let it rip, knowing it would be their last song on stage. As usual, there were no farewells at the end of the concert. The Beatles got into an armored car and left as speedily as possible. They boarded a plane back to Los Angeles, and as George sat down, he said, "That's it. I'm not a Beatle anymore."

Brian Epstein had not been at the final concert, although he hoped to change their minds about performing again. His briefcase—containing $20,000 in cash, barbiturates, and the tour contracts—had been stolen from his room in the Beverly Hills Hotel. He had received a ransom note threatening exposure of his drug habit. Nat Weiss, whose briefcase had also been stolen, went to the police. The police found the briefcases in the possession of Epstein's boyfriend, Dizz Gillespie. Around $10,000 was missing, but Epstein decided not to press charges, because he did not want his sexuality or reliance on drugs to be exposed during any investigation.

Back at London Airport on August 31, Paul was asked, "What are you planning to do today?" and he replied, "Sleep . . . sleep." All told, the Beatles had performed together around 1,400 times, and now it was all over. Meanwhile, the Cyrkle had a gig in the Catskills with only a small audience, including someone tapping on a glass and yelling, "Keep it down, I'm trying to eat in here."

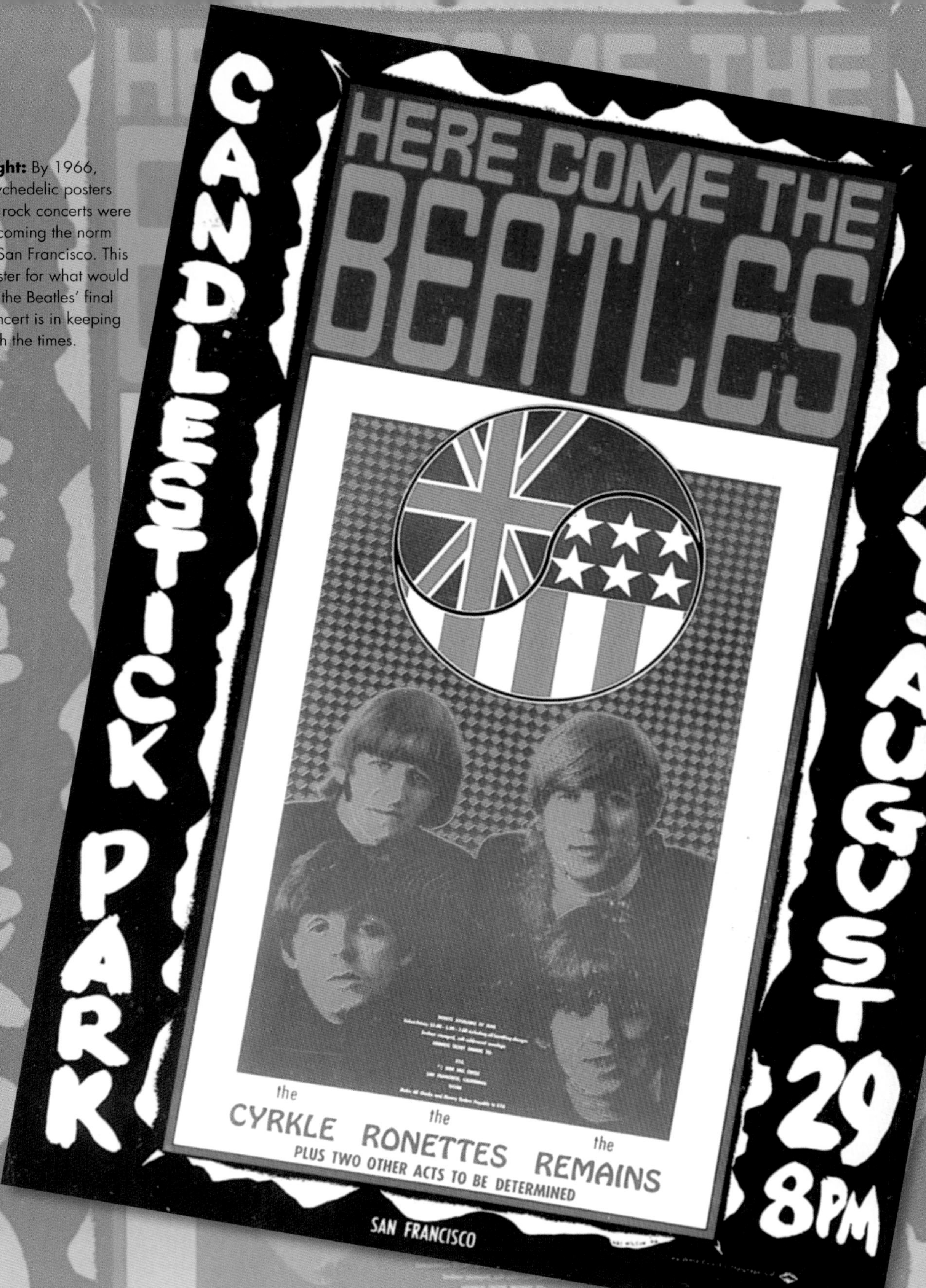

Right: By 1966, psychedelic posters for rock concerts were becoming the norm in San Francisco. This poster for what would be the Beatles' final concert is in keeping with the times.

HERE COME THE BEATLES

CANDLESTICK PARK

MONDAY. AUGUST 29 8PM

the CYRKLE
the RONETTES
the REMAINS

PLUS TWO OTHER ACTS TO BE DETERMINED

SAN FRANCISCO

The dream is over: the Beatles complete their
U.S. tour at Candlestick Park, San Francisco
and no more dates have been scheduled.
Their press officer Tony Barrow said, "Besides
all the controversy, they had had enough of
touring and they knew this tour would be
their last. After Candlestick Park, George
Harrison got on the plane and said, 'That's it.
I'm not a Beatle anymore'."

7 FROM THE SUMMER OF LOVE TO THE WINTER OF DISCONTENT

"In many ways, it is unrealistic for a band to be together for more than five years because everyone is pulling in different directions. It's like a marriage. A marriage is often artificially held together when the individuals don't have anything that they can relate to each other."

RICHARD THOMPSON

Left: "All You Need is Love," a Beatles single linked specifically to the Summer of Love, was seen by an estimated 400 million viewers when they performed it live on the TV program, *Our World*, on June 25, 1967—broadcast worldwide by satellite.

IN JUNE 1966 THE LOS ANGELES BAND THE MOTHERS OF INVENTION—masterminded by Frank Zappa—released their double album, the satirical and experimental *Freak Out!* It was greeted with hostility by the media and many of the public; however, to the Beatles it was clear that Frank Zappa was an excellent musician who wrote great lyrics with a strong sense of humor.

Barry Miles, who ran the hippie bookshop *Indica* in London, says, "Just after they'd done 'Penny Lane,' Paul McCartney told me that they were going to do their own *Freak Out!* It wouldn't be anything like *Freak Out!* but it would have a specific viewpoint. The new album was not going to be a set of tracks slapped together. *Freak Out!* has the overall theme of empowerment of youth and how brown shoes don't make it. The level of political comment in *Sgt. Pepper* is on the same level as *Freak Out!* although done entirely differently."

The Summer of Love in 1967 can be seen as a spiritual quest by the young, which involved mind-expanding drugs (specifically LSD), highly colorful clothes, and sexual freedom. The philosophy and lifestyle of LSD advocate Dr. Timothy Leary, and the availability of contraceptive pills were important factors. The media reported the happenings (and the Happenings) in New York and San Francisco.

If the engine for the Summer of Love was in San Francisco, numerous Californian groups provided the pistons. The Doors were from Los Angeles, but had some well-remembered appearances at the San Francisco Matrix Club in 1967; other San Francisco rising stars of the time were the Grateful Dead, Country Joe and the Fish, Jefferson Airplane, and Big Brother and the Holding Company (with Janis Joplin).

But the record that encapsulated and then transcended the spirit of the Summer of Love was English—the Beatles in their new guise as *Sgt. Pepper's Lonely Hearts Club Band*. They were experimenting with a creative use of time signatures, instrumentation, and lyrics. The noted theater and arts critic Kenneth Tynan called the album "a decisive moment in the history of western civilization." Tynan was using hyperbole to get noticed, but indeed, the album's size and scope were remarkable.

FIFTY CENTS · Essay: THE MERITS OF SPECULATION · SEPTEMBER 22, 1967 · TIME · THE BEATLES / Their New Incarnation · VOL 90 NO. 12

ALL YOU NEED IS LOVE

The Beatles' international influence—especially in America—was as potent as ever, a fact confirmed when "All You Need Is Love" debuted on *Our World* on June 25, 1967. It was the first live global television link by satellite, and was watched by four hundred million people in twenty-six countries.

Barry Miles watched the song being written. "John knew that he had to keep the song really simple, as most of the viewers wouldn't have English as their first language or understand much at all. People were walking around the studio carrying signs that said, 'Love' in all these different languages. It was an important message for its time." When the actor Victor Spinetti asked John what was his best lyric, John said, "That's easy, Vic. 'All You Need Is Love.'"

Above: In 1967, the satirical cartoonist Gerald Scarfe worked in papier maché for the first time to create this cover for *Time* magazine. Scarfe is married to Paul's former girlfriend, the actress Jane Asher.
Opposite: The Beatles at a photo shoot before performing on *Our World*. A few weeks later, Mick Jagger and Keith Richards were arrested for drugs offences and John and Paul added their voices to the Rolling Stones' "We Love You."

British music historian Jon Savage says, "The fact that we didn't go into Vietnam made English psychedelia very different. In a way, American psychedelia is so powerful because they were reacting against the war. Group members were drafted, and it was a terrible time. The whole of psychedelic rock in America is counterpointed by these violent demonstrations against the Pentagon. People felt incredibly strongly about it, and that was a generational rallying call too."

Just a week before the *Our World* broadcast, the first great festival gathering of the psychedelic era had taken place at the Monterey International Pop Festival in California. It was coproduced by Derek Taylor, and one of

Left and below: Antiwar protests against the Vietnam War were being organized across America, shown here in Minnesota (left) and Washington DC (below). Brian Epstein was keen for the Beatles to avoid political statements, but the individual members of the band were increasingly involved in and sympathetic to the peace movement.

the organizing board was Paul McCartney, confirming his key place in the emerging counterculture. Not long after, on August 7, George Harrison famously visited the underground heartland of the Haight-Ashbury district in San Francisco, amid much media coverage and ballyhoo.

As 1967 progressed, George Harrison was the leading voice in the Beatles' becoming involved with Indian religion and mysticism. They were intrigued by transcendental meditation (TM) as promoted by a guru they had become aware of, Maharishi Mahesh Yogi. The average fan was certainly mystified, and the Beatles were in danger of leaving their audience—as well as hitherto kindred spirits like Brian Epstein and George Martin—behind.

It was while the Beatles were sitting at the feet of the Maharishi (in a week-long meditation training session in the unlikely setting of Bangor, in North Wales) that Brian Epstein was found dead at his London home, on August 27, 1967, from an overdose of barbiturates. The Beatles were encouraged by the Maharishi to have "nice thoughts" about Brian's passing, which many observers at the time felt was trivializing the event.

Left: George in the Haight-Ashbury district of San Francisco. He led the way into hippy culture and mysticism for the Beatles.
Below: Throughout their career, the Beatles were fortunate to work with excellent, superbly creative talents. Their record producer, George Martin, encouraged their development every step of the way. His fadeout for "All You Need is Love" included a snatch of Glenn Miller's "In the Mood," believing it to be out of copyright. He was wrong, and Keith Prowse Music obtained a royalty settlement.

continued on page 206

GIVE PEACE A CHANCE

In March 1969, John Lennon and Yoko Ono were married in Gibraltar. After a lunch with Salvador Dali in Paris, they initiated their first bed-in for peace, in Amsterdam.

THEY GAVE SCORES OF MEDIA INTERVIEWS and used the slogan, "Give peace a chance." They did not mind being laughed at by the world as long as they could get their message across, and John said, "Violence is what kept us from getting together for centuries."

John and Yoko wanted to hold their second bed-in in New York, where they could attempt to persuade the American people that their Government's foreign policy was wrong. However, John's visa was rejected because of a previous drug conviction from 1968. (This was also why the Beatles couldn't have played Woodstock, even if they had wished to.)

It is advisable to look at an atlas before you embark on a long journey. John and Yoko flew to the Sheraton Oceanus Hotel in the Bahamas, but John found it was too far from America for his purposes, and the humidity was not conducive to spending seven days in bed. Canada was a better bet, so they flew on to Toronto and then Montreal, where they staged their week's bed-in at the Hotel Reine-Elizabeth.

Right: John and Yoko record "Give Peace a Chance" with Tommy Smothers from the Smothers Brothers as second guitarist.

Above: As well as promoting peace, John shared a love of hallucinogenic drugs, like LSD, with Dr Timothy Leary. President Nixon called Leary "the most dangerous man in America." He spent most of the 1970s in prison or on the run, and when he died in 1996 at the age of 75, he was fascinated—hardly surprisingly—by virtual reality systems.

Right: There was never an easier time for reporters to reach John Lennon than at his bed-in in Montreal. He and Yoko gave interviews every day, either in person or on the phone, and they always gave good copy.

Gail Renard was a sixteen-year-old Beatles fan: "I lived in Montreal, where nothing ever happened, and I heard on the radio that John and Yoko were here. They were staying in a hotel in the center of town, and I thought it would be my only chance ever to see them. The hotel was surrounded by police and hundreds of fans. I walked round to the back where nobody was. There was a fire escape and so I got up to the Lennon suite. I knocked on the door and Yoko answered. I asked if I could have an interview for my school paper and she said, 'Yes,' and my world changed. It was the best interview that the school paper ever had, and John asked me to do a radio show with him, and then he said, 'We're going to be here for eight days. Would you like to stick around and help out?' He had to speak to my mother to get permission, and she agreed. The bed-in began, and I was there for all eight days, helping Derek Taylor with the press and taking care of Yoko's daughter Kyoko."

Gail Renard watched John writing "Give Peace a Chance": "John had wanted to write a peace anthem that would last for all time, and he thought this was perfect. He wrote the lyrics on a cue card so that everyone could read them, and then he asked me to write a bigger one."

John and Yoko met Dr Timothy Leary and his wife, Rosemary. Leary was infamous for promoting hallucinogenic drugs. He was planning to run for governor of California, and he asked Lennon to write a campaign song around his slogan, "Come together, join the party." Lennon did write "Come Together," which was included on *Abbey Road*, and during "Give Peace a Chance," he twice shouts, "Come together."

On June 1, 1969, they recorded "Give Peace a Chance" in Room 1742. Along with John and Yoko were some Hare Krishna devotees with their little bells, a rabbi (hence the mention in the song), Allen Ginsberg, and Petula Clark. And there was probably someone from the FBI there in disguise,

checking on the peaceniks. Although Norman Mailer and Bob Dylan are included in the lyric, they were not present.

During their bed-in, John and Yoko held press interviews—some in person in their hotel room and others over the phone. When the cartoonist Al Capp interviewed John and Yoko, the discussion became very heated and tense. Derek Taylor wanted to throw him out but John and Yoko indulged him. Capp suggested they were doing this for money and John said he could write a song with far less effort and make more money from it.

The bed-in was followed by a press conference in Ottawa and then a tourist trip to Niagara Falls—naturally, on the Canadian side.

The single was released five weeks later on July 7, under the name of the Plastic Ono Band—and John Lennon had created an instant anthem for peace, as Pete Seeger reveals: "I can't say that I knew much about the Beatles. I'd only heard a few of their songs but some of them were really great. I happened to hear 'Give Peace a Chance' from a young woman guitar-picker just two days before I was going to a big peace demonstration in Washington on November 11, 1969. When I first heard it, I thought, 'That's a namby-pamby song, it doesn't have enough bite or militancy for me.' When I got there, I was faced with half a million people and I felt I needed a slow, slow song. I hadn't learnt anything but that one phrase but I tried it and, by gosh, it worked better and better as I kept going. Brother Kirkpatrick, Peter, Paul and Mary, and Mitch Miller came up to help me out. Before we knew it, we had half a million people swaying back and forth, like a huge ballet with children on their parents' shoulders. So 'Give Peace a Chance' is a very special song for me."

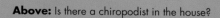

Above: Is there a chiropodist in the house?

205

LOSING THE PLOT?

In April 1967 Paul McCartney had spent some time in America with Mal Evans. Among other things, he had visited a Beach Boys' recording session and helped them with "Vegetables." He had also seen reports of Ken Kesey's Merry Pranksters, who lived and travelled on a psychedelically painted bus; this was to inspire the Beatles' TV film *Magical Mystery Tour*.

Directed by the Beatles themselves—none of whom had any real experience in filmmaking behind the camera (and it shows!)—the film featured an anarchic series of surrealist-inspired scenes that made little sense other than as "promo videos" for the musical items in the film.

Having seen how Richard Lester had directed them in *A Hard Day's Night* and *Help!*, the Beatles believed they could direct the film themselves. Their confidence was misguided and surprisingly, they didn't realize they needed some sort of a plot. Nevertheless, there are entertaining cameos and the sequences for the various songs are always well conceived.

The reviews of the hour-long TV movie were so bad that it was not picked up by any U.S. channel at the time. Its first American showing came at New York's Fillmore East (as a charity fundraiser) in August 1968, and the film wasn't seen in commercial theatres until 1974. It didn't air on U.S. television until the 1980s.

The reaction to the music was a different story on both sides of the Atlantic. "Fool on the Hill" and "I am the Walrus" are widely regarded as classics and George Harrison offered the swirling sounds of the mystical "Blue Jay Way," which is about waiting for Derek Taylor to arrive at his rented house in Los Angeles one foggy night.

In the UK, the film's music was released as a double-disc, six-track EP. In the U.S. they released an album, adding their singles from 1967, all of which had already made the number one spot ("Penny Lane," "All You Need Is Love," and "Hello Goodbye"). *Magical Mystery Tour* shot to the top of the *Billboard* charts at the end of 1967 and stayed there for eight weeks. It remained in the Top 40 for a total of thirty weeks.

Above: The Beatles in an editing suite cutting their TV film *Magical Mystery Tour*, with the film editor, Roy Benson.
Right: In 1968, the American magazine, *Look*, published as a special pull-out portfolio of the famed psychedelic portraits of the Beatles taken by the New York fashion photographer, Richard Avedon.

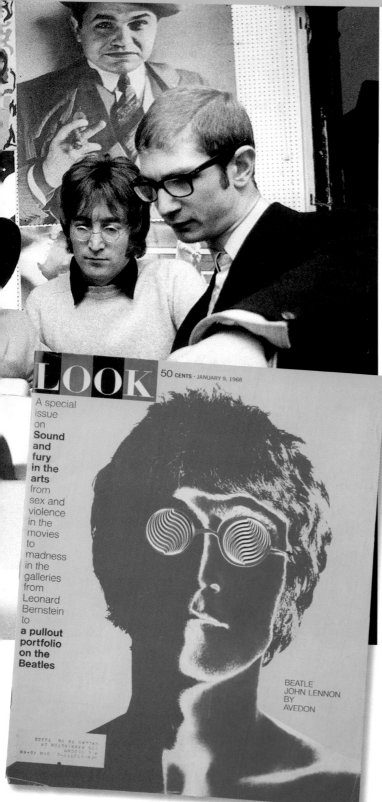

LOOK 50 CENTS · JANUARY 9, 1968

A special
issue
on
**Sound
and
fury
in the
arts**
from
sex and
violence
in the
movies
to
madness
in the
galleries
from
Leonard
Bernstein
to
**a pullout
portfolio
on the
Beatles**

BEATLE
JOHN LENNON
BY
AVEDON

Although they had ceased touring eighteen months earlier, the Beatles were still in the forefront of international news coverage when their next single, "Lady Madonna," hit the American Top 10 in March 1968. The big story in the early part of 1968 was the formation of their own record label, Apple. The first release, "Hey Jude," written by Paul for John's son Julian following the breakup of John and Cynthia's marriage, was another number one.

On the B-side of that first Apple single was "Revolution," where Lennon is looking at anarchism, but not sure whether he wants to be counted in or out. Student revolutionary Tariq Ali comments, "John had written 'Revolution' which our music critic in *Black Dwarf* described as 'pathetic'. John wrote to the magazine complaining about the review and I contacted him proposing a lengthy interview. He wondered at first if people would take him seriously but we did the interview. The next day he rang to say that he had been so inspired that he had written 'Power To The People'. John always regretted not going on anti-war demonstrations and apparently Brian Epstein had told them that anything like that would bring about a ban on them visiting the States. That was absolute nonsense as many people in the U.S. were erupting against the war as well."

Despite the qualms of the FBI, CIA and other powers-that-be, the Beatles were still the world's leading rock group. They consolidated their position with a double-album of new songs called *The Beatles*, although it was soon known as *The White Album*. The plain white sleeve, each embossed with an individual number, said it all. After the excess of *Sgt Pepper*, the Beatles had stripped down their sound—mostly to three guitarists and a drummer. Even though they had returned to basics, their songs were often quirky and mysterious.

They wrote most of the album in early 1968 while meditating with the Maharishi in Rishikesh, India. With thirty songs and a ninety-three-minute playing time, the Beatles were again expanding the boundaries for popular music and sparked a flurry of overindulgent albums by other artists, but the album that started it all worked very well, with some straightforward commercial tracks and some experimental ones—from "Ob-La-Di, Ob-La-Da" to "Revolution 9."

continued on page 214

"PAUL IS DEAD"

Nobody knows how it started, but around September 1969, American students began searching Beatles albums for clues that Paul had died, and a rumor was born.

Below: Dead or alive? If all the rumors were true, Paul was said to have died even before recording "All You Need is Love."
Opposite: A *Life* photographer tracks down Paul and Heather, alive and well in Scotland. Other magazines picked up the story—and made many column inches from the fabricated story of the rumor itself.

THE STORY MAY HAVE STEMMED from the false rumors of Bob Dylan's being killed in a motorcycle accident in 1967. The Paul rumor was equally baseless, but the first public broadcast of the information—or the first Paul-bearer, if you like—was Russ Gibb on the Detroit station WKNR-FM, talking to a student named Tom Zarski. They even played part of "Revolution 9" backwards to show that (to their ears) it sounded like "Turn me on, dead man."

THE CASE OF THE 'MISSING' BEATLE
Paul is still with us

LIFE

in this issue

PAUL McCARTNEY
The facts behind the death that wasn't

THE SEAVERS
From fastballs to fast bucks

GRAPPLING WITH OUR GARBAGE

'END OF THE ROAD'
Film shocker of the year

THE FIGHT TO BAN THE SST 'BOOM'

MAXI FASHIONS

SPECIAL BEATLES

SPECIAL BEATLES

PAUL McCARTNEY DEAD
THE GREAT HOAX

BORN 1942

DIED? 1966

COLLECTOR'S EDITION 60¢

PAUL'S MYSTERIOUS DOUBLE-- Who Is He?

THE DEATH CLUES
How The Public Found Out

THE BEATLE DEATH CURSE

WHY DID THE BEATLES KEEP PAUL'S DEATH A SECRET?

SILVER
FOX

Shelby Singleton
Music—BMI
Crawdad Music
BMI
Produced by
Bob Robin for
Shelby Singleton
Productions Inc.

12 1
711-767
Time 2:51
Arranged by
Bob & Staff

"BROTHER PAUL"
(R. Saxon–L. Capello)
BILLY SHEARS
AND THE ALL AMERICANS
A Division Of The Shelby Singleton Corp., Nashville, Tenn., U.S.A.

The program maintained that Paul McCartney had been dead for over two years—a rumor that was first reported in *The Beatles Book* in February 1967—and that the Beatles' records were strewn with clues. It started with the *Abbey Road* cover, on which Paul is out of step with his band mates—how unusual! Paul was barefoot, like a corpse (so the theory went), John in his white suit was the minister, George the gravedigger, and Ringo the funeral director.

Further "clues": Paul had his back to the camera on the back cover of *Sgt. Pepper;* John is said to mumble "I buried Paul" at the end of "Strawberry Fields Forever"; the license plate of a car on the cover of Abbey Road is 281 F and Paul would have been 28 IF he had lived; and so on. Paul denied that he was dead, but many chose not to believe him.

Beatles writer and lecturer Joel Glazier, who gives a presentation "Is Paul McCartney Dead?" says, "The *Abbey Road* cover led to the discovery of clues as to whether Paul was dead. On the front cover, Paul was the one who was out of step, Paul was the one who was barefoot, which is how people are buried in India, and Paul had his cigarette in the wrong hand. People said that a double had taken his place. These were the clues that started it, and people started to search the other albums for more clues—and found them! Some clues can be explained away, but you've still got hundreds of others to account for. Paul could have given us absolute, conclusive proof that he was still alive, but he never chose to do that."

George Martin comments, "I started getting letters about how obvious it was that Paul was dead and why were we covering it up. Paul was round at my place one afternoon and we had a good laugh about it, but it wasn't so funny to be woken in the middle of the night by some little girl in Wisconsin wanting to know if he was still alive."

Beatles' press officer Tony Barrow says, "There were rumors all through the years that one of the Beatles had been killed in a road crash or fallen off a cliff or whatever. Some of them were from fans ringing up the press so that the press would ring me and thereby find out where the Beatles were. If the press asked me if Paul was in a crash in Edinburgh, I would say, 'No, he's in Paris.' It was a fascinating story, but totally without foundation."

The *Sgt. Pepper* cover was considered another rich source for clues. On the front cover, the Beatles are standing in front of a grave. Three of the Beatles are carrying gold instruments, but Paul has a black one. Paul is wearing a badge that reads "OPD," said to be "Officially Pronounced Dead"—in fact, the badge reads "O.P.P.," which stands for Ontario Provincial Police.

Peter Blake, who created the sleeve, says, "A young boy who was helping asked if he could make a guitar in hyacinths. It seemed a nice, simple, lovely idea, so I said, 'Yes, that's fine.' If you look at the little white guitar now, you can read 'Paul?' which was one of the things around the time of the rumor that Paul was dead."

Opportunistic acts released tribute singles, such as Billy Shears and the All Americans with "Brother Paul," Terry Knight with "Saint Paul" (on Capitol, no less, and including snatches of "Hey Jude" and "A Day in the Life"), and a healthily skeptical Werbley Finster with "So Long Paul." Werbley was, in fact, José Feliciano, who made no attempt to disguise his voice.

At the time, Paul McCartney had stepped out of the public gaze and was spending time on his isolated farm in Scotland. A reporter and a photographer tracked him down, and *Life* magazine ran a cover feature, "Paul Is Still with Us," in November 1969. Paul said, "Can you just spread it around that I'm just an ordinary person who wants to live in peace?" Chances are that very few people really thought Paul was dead, but it was fun while it lasted.

Above left: The cover photograph of *Abbey Road* by Iain MacMillan was full of unintentional clues that Paul had died.
Left: "Brother Paul" by Billy Shears and the All Americans was one of several tribute singles released at the time of the "Paul is Dead" rumor.
Far left: The rumor started in February 1967 and continued to grow, despite photographic evidence, such as this shot of Paul arriving at Heathrow Airport in April 1967.

EPILOGUE

The Beatles were finished. Although they still had a record to release, the band members were happier with their solo projects and it was clear that they could no longer work together.

AN OFFICIAL ANNOUNCEMENT OF THE BEATLES' BREAKUP coincided with the release of Paul's first solo album, *McCartney*, in April 1970. The press release included an interview with McCartney that made it clear that the Beatles were no more. John was furious, as he had been making moves to leave months earlier and felt that, as he was the one who had started the group, he had the right to end it. And, in any event, the Beatles were about to release *Let It Be*.

Moving to new territory with the title *All Things Must Pass*, George Harrison went solo with a triple album that became a best-seller, topping the U.S. charts in December 1970. He went on to organize the *Concert for Bangladesh*, the first major rock event for charity, presenting two concerts in August 1971 at New York's Madison Square Garden, featuring Ravi Shankar, Bob Dylan, Leon Russell, Eric Clapton, Billy Preston, and Ringo Starr. The public hoped for a Beatles reunion, but litigation had caused a rift between Paul and the other Beatles—and John wouldn't appear without Yoko, whose presence George thought would test the audience's patience.

Having released the starkly confessional *John Lennon/Plastic Ono Band* just a week or so after George's solo debut, in September 1971 (as the

Opposite: The Beatles with Billy Preston brave the cold for a short set on the rooftop at Apple on January 30, 1969. The unannounced performance was cut short by the police and John said, "I'd like to say thank you on behalf of the group and ourselves and I hope we passed the audition." The Beatles never performed in public again.

Above: Allen Klein, Apple's financial adviser, knew how to obtain the highest royalty rates from a record company, but his self-interest and belligerence worked against him, and soon it wasn't just Paul who was regretting his presence.
Below: George Harrison and Ravi Shankar at the press conference to promote the fundraising Concert for Bangladesh.

chart-topping "Imagine" was hitting the stores) John and Yoko moved to attempt to take up residence in New York City. But because of a drug conviction, John was refused the green card that would allow him to leave and return whenever he wished. John's increasing political activity took center stage in the sloganeering *Sometime in New York City* (1972), which didn't help his profile at the FBI.

In 1973, when John and Yoko's marriage became strained, Yoko spoke to their assistant May Pang and suggested that she take John to Los Angeles. May Pang says, "She was handing over her husband to someone else. I resisted at first, but she wanted me to start that night. I was with John during his famous 'lost weekend,' which was a lot more creative than people think. The few wild incidents were blown out of proportion. He was even considering writing with Paul, and, if he hadn't gone back with Yoko, I would have pushed for it."

In all probability, Paul missed working with John more than John missed working with Paul. No matter how much hurt and public humiliation he had received from John, Paul would have forgiven everything and worked with him again. They came close to it, notably in 1974 when they were in a studio in Los Angeles with Stevie Wonder and Nilsson, but the jam session is nowhere near as enticing as it sounds.

John returned to Yoko in 1975, and Yoko gave birth to Sean on John's 35th birthday. Lennon became a house husband and kept a relatively low profile, and in 1976, after a protracted court battle, he received his green card and was told he could apply for U.S. citizenship in 1981. But that was not to be.

DEATH IN NEW YORK CITY

In June 1980, John sailed to Bermuda, where he wrote some new songs. The result, *Double Fantasy*, was released in November. The next month, on the evening of December 8, John Lennon was fatally shot in the entrance to the Dakota Building where he and Yoko lived. He'd signed a copy of his new album for his murderer earlier that night, and he was an easy target because he wasn't surrounded by bodyguards. His final words were "Yes, I'm John Lennon."

John's death triggered an outpouring of grief, not least in New York City, where he had made his home and met his

Left: John Lennon outside the court room in August 1974. Inside, he claimed that the attempt to have him deported was nothing to do with his drug conviction in 1968, and everything to do with his stance against the Vietnam war.

IMAGINE

Far left: A couple grieving for John Lennon in Central Park, New York, holding a picture of John and Yoko at a bed-in.
Below: It seemed that every newspaper and magazine had its take on John Lennon's life and death. Today the name of John Lennon's killer is omitted from most books on the grounds that he killed him for his own notoriety.

death. A small plot of land in Central Park, just adjacent to the Dakota Building, was renamed "Strawberry Fields," and remains a permanent memorial, with the word "Imagine" spelled out in mosaic tiles.

Over the following years, the three surviving Beatles were inextricably involved with the United States, both professionally and in their personal lives. Paul McCartney's lavish stage shows, performed in huge arenas across America (and the rest of the world), have become increasingly Beatlecentric, with up to 60 percent of his repertoire now covers of Beatles classics.

Paul's personal connections with the U.S. have been cemented by the fact that two of his three marriages have been to Americans: Linda Eastman (until her death in 1998) and his current wife, Nancy Shevell. And he still maintains homes in the

JOHN LENNON
HIS LIFE AND TIMES
A 16-page retrospective

16-page pullout on John Lennon's life
Tonight
Killer stalked him 3 days
EXCLUSIVE: Lennon & suspect

DAILY N
100,000 J
LENNON VIG

DAILY NEWS
JOHN'S WILL: $30M PLUS
Half to Yoko, rest to trust

Ron to bare 8 cabinet picks today
Angry Jean stalks out diet doc tr

Lennon's last interview
riders face delays
City's coolest judges

United States—one in New York and another, a ranch near Tucson, Arizona.

In 1988, George's inherent good nature came through on his sensational collaborative album with Jeff Lynne, Tom Petty, Bob Dylan, and Roy Orbison, *The Travelling Wilburys, Vol. 1*, although the follow-up—without Orbison, who by that time had died—was less impressive. After a long battle with cancer, George died in Los Angeles in November 2001, and since then the contribution he made to the Beatles has been increasingly appreciated.

For several years Ringo—who has been married to an American, Barbara Bach, since 1981—had a run of hit singles and albums in the United States. He recorded *Beaucoups of Blues* (1970) in Nashville with top-name country musicians, and his engaging *Ringo* (1973) almost topped the *Billboard* album charts. The problem for Ringo was how to fill his time, and he found the answer with his acclaimed All-Starr Band. It's a greatest hits concert, as the musicians play Ringo's successes as well as their own.

Although John's death laid to rest any talk of a complete Beatles reunion, it also led to a massive reissue program. The first volume of *Anthology* (1995), a double CD of unissued takes, sold thirteen million copies worldwide. And also in 1995, all three surviving Beatles released

"Free as a Bird" and "Real Love," recorded in 1994 using John's home demo tapes from 1977—a digital reunion of the Fab Four, twenty-five years after their disbandment. In 2000, the hits collection *1* sold thirty-one million copies. There has been endless repackaging of the Beatles' back catalogue, including replicas of the 1960s American albums on CD.

Half a century after their domination of popular music on a global scale, the name of the Beatles is still universally recognized. And back in the '60s, that domination was achieved through their unparalleled acceptance in the land where their music—rock 'n' roll in its many manifestations—

Opposite page left: Ringo married his very own Bond girl, Barbara Bach, in 1981.
Opposite page right: Paul and Linda McCartney on their wedding day in 1969. Linda was a rock photographer at the time, best known for the pictures she took of Jimi Hendrix.
Above: And they were right ... Beatles fans greet their idols outside the Plaza Hotel in New York, February 1964.

began: the United States of America. As the four members of the biggest pop group ever were always first to acknowledge, without America and its musical heritage there simply would have been no Beatles in the first place.

221

PHOTO CREDITS

Key: t = top; b = bottom; l = left; r = right; c = center

Alamy/Celebrity: 126; **/flab:** 185b; **/Globe Photos/Zuma Press:** 89; **/Andrew Hasson:** 189b; **/Della Huff:** 21; **/Keystone Pictures USA:** 166; **/M&N:** 184tr; **/Marc Tielemans:** 210tr; **/Moviestore Collections:** 185t; **/Pictorial Press Ltd.:** 26l, 79r, 85t, 86/87, 91, 202/203, 205, 212/213; **/Trinity Mirror/Mirrorpix:** 16t, 67, 74/75, 78, 96/97, 113b, 114, 123, 206/207; **Zuma Press/Globe Photos/Rick Mackler:** 68

Beatles Book Picture Library: 71t

© 2013 Bill Bernstein: 6

Camera Press London/Curt Gunther: 125t, 129, 136/137, 154; **/MPTV:** 155 main, 155 inset

Corbis/Bettmann: 37, 54, 105t, 107t, 109tl, 122l, 142/143, 148t, 164/165, 175b, 187l, 200b, 201l, 204b, 218bl, 223; **/Bettmann/UPI/Bob Flora:** 117b; **/Classicstock:** 14; **/Amy Harris:** 45b; **/Michael Levin:** 29c; **/Minnesota Historical Society:** 200t; **/Reuters:** 201r

FBI Report Subject: The Beatles, Denver Extortion investigation, File number 9-42653: 120

Getstock/Boris Spremo: 127

Getty Images: 7, 69t, 210l; **/Fiona Adams/Redferns:** 12/13; **/Authenticated News:** 95b; **/Camerique:** 26r; **/CBS Photo Archive:** 51, 52l; **/Central Press:** 16b; **Cummings Archive:** 220r; **/Evening Standard:** 82r; **/Express:** 216; **Express/Harry Benson:** 92, 109tr, 110/111; **/Fox Photos:** 36, 145; **/Frank Driggs Collection:** 20; **/Gamma Keystone:** 72; **/Bernard Gotfryd:** 8/9, 43, 49t; **/Ken Harding/BIPS:** 17; **/Mark & Colleen Hayward:** 159b; **/Hulton Archive/Central Press:** 86l; **Hulton Archive/Keystone Features:** 86l; **/Hulton Archive/William Lovelace:** 76, 105b, 111t, 112; **Hulton Archive Rowland Scherman:** 56/57; **Hulton Archive/Robert Whitaker:** 153r, 153l, 156, 183; **/Keystone:** 83t; **/Keystone/Evan Agostini:** 219; **/Keystone/Luiz Alberto:** 218tr; **/NBCU Photobank:** 184b; **/New York Daily News Archive/Dan Farrell:** 149; **New York Daily News Archive/Fred Morgan:** 221; **New York Daily News Archive/Hyman Rothman:** 189t; **New York Daily News Archive/Frank Russo:** 140t,140b,141; **Terry O'Neill:** 220l; **/Michael Ochs Archives:** 22, 29r, 44, 45t, 52r, 53, 62t, 87r, 93, 94, 115br, 116, 118, 153r, 169b, 196/197; **/Popperfoto:** 28, 47, 48, 60, 60/61, 63, 77, 144, 217t, 217b; **David Redferns:** 199; **/Redferns/GAB Archives:** 25b, 29l, 79l, 85b, 90, 193; **Redferns/Chris Morphet:** 35; **Redferns/Gilles Petard:** 95t, 102, 169t; **Redferns/Visualeyes Archive:** 88; **/Retrofile/George Marks:** 18r; **/SSPL/Daily Herald Archive:** 27; **Bob Thomas:** 19t; **/Time Life Pictures/Don Cravens:** 102/103, 107t; **/Time Life Pictures/Bob Gomel:** 70b; **Time Life Pictures/Burton McNeely:** 133b, 134

© Mark Hayward Archive: 160/161

Fred Hoyt: 130, 131bl, 132t, 132b

Spencer Leigh: 210br

Bradley Loos: 19b

David Marks / 3rd Ear's Hidden years Music Archive, South Africa > www.3rdearmusic.com: 173b

© Jim Marshall: 194/195

Don McLaughlin: 131tl, 131tr, 131br

Minnesota History Center/St Paul Dispatch and Pioneer Press/Sully: 156/157

Mark Naboshek: 23b,23t, 34, 58/59, 65b, 65t, 69b, 71b, 73b, 73t, 81, 82l, 83b, 109b, 115tl, 139tr, 139br, 146l, 146r, 148b, 150, 152l, 157r, 158bl, 158tr, 162, 163, 170, 173t, 176, 177, 178, 179l, 179r, 182tl, 182r, 188t, 188b, 191r, 198, 207bl, 209t, 209b, 215

PA Photos/AP: 11, 120/121, 138/139, 151, 171 main, 171 inset, 172, 174l, 175t, 180/181, 190/191, 214; **AP/Mike Mitchell:** 56b, 56tl 56tr; **/Canadian Press Images/Montreal Gazette:** 204t; **/Charles Tasnadi:** 42; **Rex Features:** 208; **/Dezo Hoffmann:** 46

Edward Delos Santos/PinoyKollektor.blogspot.com: 167

Shutterstock: 64, 121, 218/219

Topfoto: 15t, 18l; **/Topham Picturepoint:** 15b

Toronto Star: 30r, 31l, 31r, 32, 33

Tracks Images: 2/3, 38/39, 40t, 40/41, 41t, 49b, 50, 55b, 58, 62b, 70t, 80, 98, 99l, 99r, 108, 113t, 117t, 122r, 124bl, 124tr, 125bl, 125br, 133t, 138t, 138b, 174r, 182bl, 187br

University of North Texas Libraries/Museum of the Gulf Coast, Port Arthur, Texas: 119

V&A Images/Harry Hammond: 25t

Pip Wedge: 30l

Yorkspace/Bruce McFadden: 128t; **/Madison Sale:** 128b

Every effort has been made to trace the copyright holders of the artworks in this book. In order for any errors or omissions to be corrected in future editions, please contact Elephant Book Company.

ACKNOWLEDGMENTS

The author and publisher would like to thank the following people for their assistance in producing this book:
Anne Leigh, Mark Lewisohn, Mark Naboshek, and Mary-Lu Zahalan.

With the exception of the Beatles, all quoted interviews were conducted by the author, often for BBC Radio Merseyside. Thank you to all concerned.

Many thanks to Robert Greeson for his assistance in photographing items of memorabilia from the collection of Mark Naboshek.

BIBLIOGRAPHY

Many books (I own over three hundred of them!) have been consulted while writing this book, including the following:

The Beatles Forever – Nicholas Schaffner (Cameron House, 1977)
Be My Baby – Ronnie Spector with Vince Waldron (Harmony, 1990)
The Beatles off the Record – Keith Badman (Omnibus, 2000)
Not Just the Beatles – Sid Bernstein with Arthur Aaron (Jacques & Flusster, 2000)
The Beatles Are Coming! – Bruce Spizer (498 Productions, 2003)
The Bootleg Guide – Garry Freeman (Scarecrow, 2003)
Ticket to Ride – Larry Kane (Running Press, 2003)
John, Paul, George, Ringo, & Me – Tony Barrow (Andre Deutsch, 2005)
Meet the Beatles – Steven D. Stark (HarperCollins, 2005)
The Beatles: Film & TV Chronicle – Jörg Pieper & Volker Path (Premium, 2005)
The Unreleased Beatles – Richie Unterberger (Backbeat, 2006)
The Gospel According to the Beatles – Steve Turner (Westminster John Knox, 2006)
Can't Buy Me Love: The Beatles, Britain, and America – Jonathan Gould (Harmony, 2007)
Beatles for Sale – John Blaney (Jawbone, 2008)
Sundays with Sullivan – Bernie Ilson (Taylor Trade, 2009)
Complete Beatles Chronicle – Mark Lewisohn (Hamlyn, 1992)

Front cover, top left: Screaming fans wait for the Beatles outside the Delmonico Hotel in New York in August 1964, during their first North American tour. (Getty Images/NY Daily News Archive/Arthur Buckley)
Top right: The Beatles step off the plane to a rapturous reception as they arrive in America for the first time, February 7, 1964. (Getty Images/Michael Ochs Archives)
Bottom right: The band toured vast venues in the U.S., including Shea Stadium, home of the Mets baseball team. (Getty Images/Michael Ochs Archives)
Bottom center: A photo shoot in Central Park, February 1964 (George was suffering with a sore throat and stayed in the hotel). (Getty Images/Paul Popper/Popperfoto)
Bottom left: The Beatles performing on *The Ed Sullivan Show* in New York City, on February 9, 1964. (Getty Images/Paul Popper/Popperfoto)

Back cover, left: The Beatles subathing at the Deauville Hotel, Miami, during their first U.S. visit, in 1964. (Getty Images/Time Life Pictures/Bob Gomel)
Right: A promotional shot of the Beatles taken before their first North American tour, in 1964; their success in the U.S. opened doors for many other British bands. (Alamy/Trinity Mirror/Mirrorpix)

Previous page: More than 55,000 fans were at the Beatles' Shea Stadium concert on August 15, 1965. could hear the roar of the crowd for miles around.